Advance Praise for AARP Meditations for Caregivers

"Drawing on their personal and professional experience, Barry Jacobs and Julia Mayer provide caregivers with a fine assortment of stories and meditations to meet the emotional challenges of family caregiving. This invaluable, wise, and compassionate guide is frank, inspirational, and altogether timelessly human."
—John S. Rolland, MD, Professor of Psychiatry and Behavioral Sciences, Northwestern University Feinberg School of Medicine

"*AARP Meditations for Caregivers* is filled with stories of hope, perseverance—even transcendence. Drawing from their personal experience as well as others, Drs. Jacobs and Mayer remind us that providing care for a loved one can be a sacred, moral, and enriching endeavor."
—Katy Butler, author of *Knocking on Heaven's Door*

"This collection of lessons and insights assures us that our caregiving experiences are not unique. Stressed caregivers will be able to draw solace from these anecdotes."
—Robert L. Kane, MD, School of Public Health, University of Minnesota, and author of *The Good Caregiver*

"This book will help caregivers find their own way to a place of calm and purposefulness. In *AARP Meditations for Caregivers*, clinical psychologists Barry Jacobs and Julia Mayer help caregivers understand and accept their wide-ranging emotions—from anxiety and resentment to devotion and forgiveness. The concise meditations combine simple but powerful storytelling with compassionate insights gained from the authors' personal and professional experience."
—Carol Levine, director, Families and Health Care Project, United Hospital Fund, and author of *Planning for Long-Term Care For Dummies*

"This book is truly a bible for caregivers. Barry Jacobs and Julia Mayer tell more than 100 stories of dilemmas faced by children, siblings, husbands, and wives thrust into the role of caregiver. The psychotherapists follow up each tale with a simple, powerful nugget of advice. Reading these all-too-human tales, caregivers won't feel quite as alone—and they'll see that even when they're angry, frustrated, sad, and stressed out, they can find ways to express love, empathy, and humor."

—Marc Silver, author of *Breast Cancer Husband: How to Help Your Wife (And Yourself) Through Diagnosis, Treatment, and Beyond*

"*AARP Meditations for Caregivers* captures the frustrations and determination, sorrows, and joys typically experienced by family caregivers. Drs. Jacobs and Mayer offer concrete suggestions and inspiration for those who provide countless acts of loving care."

—Janis Abrahms Spring, PhD,
author of *Life with Pop: Lessons on Caring for an Aging Parent*

"As a son caring for my mother for more than five years, I wish this insightful and inspirational book was available five years ago. I was deeply moved by the passages."

—Louis G. Colbert, MSW, Vice President of Operations,
Philadelphia Corporation for Aging, and Past Chair,
American Society for Aging Board of Directors

"This book should be a companion for every family caregiver. In *AARP Meditations for Caregivers*, Dr. Barry Jacobs and Dr. Julia Mayer have created an inspirational and useful tool for caregivers as we navigate the challenging emotional road of caregiving. The real-life caregiver stories in the book will resonate, and the practical tips for coping are quick and relevant."

—Amy Goyer, caregiver and author of *Juggling Life, Work, and Caregiving*

"How we take care of our old and our young defines us as individuals and as a people. Jacobs and Mayer take on the complex matter of caring for ourselves while caring for our loved ones with expertise, compassion, and artistry."

—Steven E. Arnold, MD, Translational Neurology Head,
Interdisciplinary Brain Center, Massachusetts General Hospital,
Harvard Medical School

"There are few more difficult or important tasks in life than that of caregiving. This book by two family psychologists who specialize in working with caregivers provides just the right mix of inspiration, advice, meditations, and exemplary stories to help us make the experience helpful and healing."
—Susan H. McDaniel, PhD, Dr. Laurie Sands Distinguished Professor of Families & Health, University of Rochester Medical Center

"I'm delighted to have this resource available for the caregivers we see in our clinic—and for my own bedside table. Taking time to reflect on the depths of our feelings about caregiving is often at the bottom of the to-do list. This book offers the opportunity to ponder, explore, reflect, and accept one big challenging feeling in a way that makes it seem manageable."
—Sara Honn Qualls, Director, Gerontology Center, University of Colorado Colorado Springs, and coauthor of *Caregiver Family Therapy*

"While developing and implementing a long-term plan by and for aging parents is critical to the long-term health of the family, equally important is meeting the psychological and spiritual needs of the caregivers of those parents along the way. This book does a very effective job of fulfilling those ongoing needs."
—Tim Prosch, author of *The Other Talk: A Guide to Talking with Your Adult Children about the Rest of Your Life*

"This inspired book directly addresses and celebrates the longstanding, complex, and often challenging family caregiving relationships that emerge in the face of difficult circumstances. Through short anecdotes, the authors present readily identifiable and sometimes humorous difficulties as well as practical solutions that are likely to resonate with all walks of caregivers."
—Jennifer Wolff, PhD, Associate Professor, Center on Aging and Health, Johns Hopkins University

AARP Meditations for Caregivers

AARP®
Real Possibilities

Meditations
for Caregivers

Practical, Emotional, and Spiritual Support
for You and Your Family

BARRY J. JACOBS, PsyD, and JULIA L. MAYER, PsyD

Da Capo
∞
LIFE
LONG

Design and composition by Eclipse Publishing Services
Set in 11-point Brioso Pro

Library of Congress Control Number: 2016014781

First Da Capo Press edition 2016

ISBN: 978-0-7382-1902-8 (paperback)
ISBN: 978-0-7382-1903-5 (e-book)

Published by Da Capo Press, an imprint of Perseus Books,
a division of PBG Publishing, LLC, a subsidiary of Hachette Book Group, Inc.
www.dacapopress.com

Sources for the quotes that appear at the start of each chapter can be found on page 213

A range of AARP print and e-books is available at AARP's online bookstore, aarp.org/bookstore, and through local and online bookstores.

Da Capo Press books are available at special discounts for bulk purchases in the U.S. by corporations, institutions, and other organizations. For more information, please contact the Special Markets Department at 2300 Chestnut Street, Suite 200, Philadelphia, PA, 19103, or call (800) 810-4145, ext. 5000, or e-mail special.markets@perseusbooks.com.

10 9 8 7 6 5 4 3 2 1

*This book is dedicated in loving memory to
Renee, Joe, and Morton*

Contents

Acknowledgments

To family caregivers who are doing the hard work every day. Your dedication, love, and devotion make the world a better place.

To our psychotherapy clients who have shared your stories with us over the years, many of which are in this book. We are honored to have been witness to your efforts.

To our friends and family members who have shared your own caregiving stories, some of which are in this book, and who have supported us both in our caregiving efforts and in the writing of this book. Thank you. Your support means so much to us.

To Bill Warning, MD; Christine Donohue-Henry, MD; and the residents, faculty members, and staff of the Crozer-Keystone Center for Family Health in Springfield, Pennsylvania. It has been a privilege to strive together with you to partner with our primary care patients and their family members.

To Monica and Aaron. You have been indispensable. Thank you for your help and support. We love you.

To Jodi Lipson. Thank you for conceiving this book and for choosing us to write it. Your editing, thoughtful comments, and support made all the difference. To Tom Miller. Thank you for all you've done to move this book forward. You managed complex situations, quelled our numerous anxieties, and offered your wisdom, all while remaining patient and kind. To Dan Ambrosio. Thank you for believing in this project and for making it happen. What a pleasure to work with all of you. Thank you for giving us this opportunity.

Introduction

Throughout our years of caring for our aging parents, we have lived with the fear of falling. Literally and figuratively. Barry's frail, elderly mother, Jean, frequently forgot to use her walker, lost her balance, and went down hard in her apartment a mile from our suburban Philadelphia home. Each time we visited her, we wondered if we would find her on the floor. Each time our house phone rang, we half-expected to hear the voice of one of her aides or a police officer or a nurse telling us she'd been transported to the emergency room. As she fell with greater frequency, our spirits fell, too.

It could have been a warm, sunny morning when we might have preferred to take a leisurely walk together through the nearby woods, something we've enjoyed doing many times in our twenty-five years of marriage. But we'd have no time for morning coffee, a glance at the newspaper, or even much discussion. We'd jump in the car and rush to the hospital. Our day would then be spent in the dreary ER cubicle where Jean's delicate skin would get bandaged, her back would be x-rayed, and her mental state evaluated. There'd be CT scans and blood tests and hours and hours of sitting around awaiting test results. Caring for her was anything but a walk in the woods.

Our story isn't unusual or special. More people are caring for aging parents, disabled spouses, and chronically ill children every year. According to *Caregiving in the U.S. 2015*, a report by the National Alliance for Caregiving and AARP, 40 million Americans now provide unpaid care to cherished family members or friends each year. We, like many, have chosen to care for our loved ones as much as we are capable. The fact that we are clinical psychologists who special-ize in working with family caregivers gives us few advantages, though, when caring for our own family members. We can anticipate or ana-lyze our own emotional reactions but rarely prevent them.

Jean has always been a highly opinionated, controlling, determined woman, albeit one with charm, style, and a sense of humor. Caring for her for the past five years (like caring for Julia's father, Joe, eight years ago, and later, Barry's stepfather, Steve) has been stressful in many ways. With each of these challenges that we've overcome or at least endured, we have learned.

We've learned that compassion helps. When we are most frus-trated, we put ourselves in Jean's position and try to imagine what we would feel like if we were her. We slow down, speak respectfully, and always try to explain what we want, what we are doing, what we are hoping for, so that she can join with us in common effort to help her live as well as possible. Later, we take the time to express our feelings to one another and offer each other encouragement. We acknowledge our own limitations, whether physical or emotional, and find ways to work around them. We remember to look at the big picture. Even though a difficult day can feel overwhelming, we know that this time of our lives is limited. We try to see the crises as challenges to our cre-ativity and look for innovative solutions when we can.

We don't deny that family caregiving is hard, worrisome work. But, over time, the process has also offered up some surprisingly inspira-tional and positive experiences for each of us. When a challenging day goes well, we feel especially competent and a bit more confident in our abilities. We frequently find novel solutions to irksome problems. When laughing or reminiscing together, we feel a shared sense of joy and an increased appreciation of the humor in some situations. By practicing compassion, we've grown in our ability to take another per-son's perspective, respect his or her needs and wishes, and construc-tively overcome trying circumstances.

With an increased awareness of the fragility of life, we often find ourselves feeling grateful for an opportunity to make Jean happy or meet her needs. We feel grateful that we have enough good health ourselves that we can be of service to her. By assuming a mindful stance toward each day's tasks, we find ourselves feeling more grateful for other aspects of our lives, such as our terrific kids and our relationship with one another.

We discovered that caregiving is meaningful to us in many ways. It helps define the type of people we aspire to be. As exhausted as we feel at times, we take solace in the fact that we are doing good work. That has always been an important value to us. We are glad for the chance to demonstrate that value to our children through caring for their grandparents.

After a particularly rough stretch during which Jean had been repeatedly hospitalized for falls, she and we decided that she would move into a nursing home. She is safer there now, experiencing fewer falls. Our family caregiving hasn't ended because we continue to try to help her in that setting as much as we can. But our days of running to her apartment to lift her off the floor or rushing to the ER are now over. Our fear of falling has eased, and we are feeling more grounded in the knowledge that we've all made a prudent decision together.

With this book, we hope to share all that we've learned, from our own and others' experiences, about caring for loved ones in their homes as well as in hospitals and nursing homes. We suggest ways that caregiving can provide you with similarly transformative experiences and a sense of belonging to a larger caregiving community. We want to give you a long view of the benefits of providing loving care to encourage you to persevere in this vital work. To achieve all this, we've combined several elements:

- We've drawn on the power of stories to illuminate, inspire, and instruct. With nearly each one of the 152 meditations here, we tell the tale of a real-life family struggling with the emotional and logistical challenges of caregiving and enlightening lessons learned in the process. Some of these stories stem from our personal experiences as well as those of our extended family members. Most of them are stories we were privileged to hear from our psychotherapy clients during the past twenty-five years; the names and other details of these clients have been changed to protect their identities.

- We've organized the stories into twenty-eight themes—including anger, anxiety, guilt, commitment, optimism, and respect—that capture many of the experiences of the hardworking caregivers we've met.

- Throughout the book, we have incorporated the insights and techniques of stress management and mindfulness that are at the core of so much of today's psychological practice, including our own. We believe strongly that, to the degree that caregivers can pay attention to the tenderness and love in their interactions with care receivers, they will be enriched and heartened by caregiving.

We hope that these meditations will provide you with solutions to typical caregiving challenges, offer relief and renewal through mindfulness, and inspire you to find the meaning and value in the work you do. We hope you are moved by the stories here and that you share your own stories with other caregivers. They, too, need support, validation, and a positive perspective on this challenging time in their lives.

CHAPTER 1

Accept Your Feelings

For after all, the best thing one can do when it is raining
is let it rain.
—Henry Wadsworth Longfellow

One of the greatest challenges we face as humans is truly accepting that we are human, difficult feelings and all. We struggle with our rage, shame, guilt, and disappointment, and we glory in our intense love and devotion. As caregivers, at times we are likely to feel an overwhelming, contradictory array of emotions. Current experiences trigger old feelings. New worries remind us of old situations. How should we handle whatever emotions come up? We can try to accept them, understanding that they are just feelings. They rise up, we experience them, and then they pass. They are evidence of our humanity.

When you have difficult feelings, don't judge them.

Instead, approach them with curiosity, compassion, and interest.

1. Take the time to notice exactly what you are feeling. Are you angry, scared, ashamed, disappointed, or longing for some care?

2. Reflect upon those feelings. Are they intense and lasting, or are they more moderate and passing? Do you feel them in your body as well as in your mind? Where in your body?

3. What triggered the feelings? Was it something someone said or did? Was it a thought or worry that you had?

4. Have memories been stirred up? Can you make a connection between the current feelings and other occasions in which you felt the same way?

5. Consider what you'd like to do about the feelings. What would you like to accomplish? Do you want to communicate them to someone? If so, what would be the most effective way to do that? Would you prefer to keep them to yourself or to express them in a creative way? Write about them? Draw a picture? Dance?

Taking the time to reflect allows us to have our feelings rather than to have them overtake us. We can then explore the most useful ways to manage them. We are more likely to discover flexible, creative approaches to the management and expression of our feelings if we have patiently made the effort to gain some perspective on them.

After several sleepless nights in a row filled with tossing and turning and racing thoughts, Howard decided that he had to talk to his wife.

Before bed on the following night, he sat down with Sherri and told her how terrible he felt about sometimes wishing that his father would die. He said that he loved his father. Then he hung his head in shame and cried.

They'd been caring for his father for several years, during which his health had declined sharply. His dementia was putting a strain on the whole family—so much planning, putting out fires, and covering the expenses. Howard was worried about their future financial stability.

Sherri gave him a hug. She loved Howard's dad, too. She knew how hard it was for Howard to say those words aloud. She reassured him that anyone in his situation would have those feelings from time to time. She admitted to sometimes having the same wish.

Both felt relieved that they'd shared their feelings. Howard felt understood. He felt relieved. And he was able to get to sleep more easily that night.

Rather than judging our thoughts and feelings, we can try to accept them and show compassion toward ourselves. We are only human.

BARRY:

There were times while caring for my mother when I didn't seem to do anything right.

I procrastinated in scheduling her next medical appointment, and then her doctor went on a long vacation. I forgot to pick up her pills from the pharmacy, so she had to go a day without her blood pressure medicine. I grew impatient with her too often and hurt her feelings.

My failings embarrassed me. I judged myself harshly: I was an inadequate son, a reprobate caregiver. She deserved better. I was sure other caregiving sons were more competent and composed. I was letting both of us down.

My mother could sense that I was struggling with myself. She said multiple times, "I'm sorry this is so hard." Her words made me feel guilty, in part, but also gave me some comfort. She really understood that this journey we were on together was hard. There were many appointments to make, meals to organize, supplies to order. She accepted that I would botch things at times. She never once criticized me.

Her acceptance of me helped spur my self-acceptance. I realized I was an imperfect son before I became her caregiver; I would always be an imperfect caregiving son. Self-criticism didn't improve my performance. I had to accept who I was and what I could and couldn't do. I even had to accept my own frustrations. I was doing my best and that was good enough for my mother. She was giving me a pass, perhaps, but then again, she always did.

We need to be kind and understanding toward ourselves
as much as we are compassionate toward those we care for.

After Nora and Tom's mother died, Nora wanted to feel closer to her older brother.

They were six years apart, and although they got along, they weren't especially close. They spoke easily about their father, who was now living by himself and needed some support from them. They complained that he avoided going to doctors' appointments and wasn't eating right or exercising enough. They could laugh about how stubborn he was. This was a point of connection for them.

But they couldn't talk easily about their mother. When the topic of conversation turned to her, Nora would inevitably cry and Tom would become irritated. He would express his impatience with her emotion and quickly get off the phone. Nora would feel terrible that she couldn't share her feelings with her only sibling. She felt that the reason was because he was avoiding his own feelings. The emotional distance between Nora and Tom felt huge.

After their father passed away, things changed. Tom was overcome with his emotions. He and his wife had three children by then. Tom couldn't help but feel the pain of the loss. Nora took the opportunity to try to connect with him again. This time, Tom was patient and accepting when Nora became emotional. He didn't exactly cry with her, but he no longer ran from the feelings. Because they could share their emotions more, they were able to develop the closer relationship Nora had longed for.

Sharing our painful feelings with our loved ones brings us closer to them and helps us to process our emotions together.

Trudy had spent her lifetime trying but failing to please her hypercritical mother, Louise.

Even as a young girl, she had tried to be as good as gold, jumping to Louise's every request. Now that Louise was aging and hobbled with constant arthritic pain, Trudy found herself repeating the old pattern, waiting for Louise's directions. With one word of praise from her mother, Trudy felt uplifted. But if Louise were cross or even silent—perhaps due to the severe pain she was experiencing—then Trudy felt chided.

After months of this kind of caregiving, Trudy felt physically and emotionally exhausted. It wasn't just her recent efforts that had drained her; she felt wrung dry by decades of striving. Feeling so tired made her feel guilty and ashamed, as if she were still failing to be the daughter her mother wanted. Feeling ashamed, in turn, made her feel depressed. She was trapped in this negative cycle of emotions.

At her husband's urging, she sought the services of a psychotherapist. Through therapy, she gleaned a simple but important insight: Because of the type of person that Louise was, it wasn't possible for Trudy or anyone to always please her. This insight was liberating. Trudy could continue to try her best to help her mother because she truly loved her and didn't want to see her suffer. But she had to accept that she couldn't control her mother's response.

Trudy continued to work hard on Louise's behalf. But she stopped beating herself up when she failed to win Louise over. She didn't have to prove herself anymore.

Some caregivers attempt to win love and approval from family members who've rejected them for years. Judge your efforts on their own merits and not in hopes of receiving others' positive responses.

CHAPTER 2

Anger or Resentment

If you are patient in one moment of anger, you will escape a hundred days of sorrow.
—Chinese proverb

We always start with good intentions, but sometimes situations become stressful and our best-laid plans go awry. Naturally, anger rears its head occasionally when we care for our loved ones. Rather than beat ourselves up, or sink into shame, we can reflect on our anger as an opportunity for growth. We can challenge ourselves to feel more empathy for our loved ones, discover the sadness behind our angry feelings, and develop as dedicated caregivers, open to learning more about our loved ones and ourselves in the process of providing loving care.

As children, they always were protective of their little brother.

As adults, they were now ready to pounce on him. Clara, the older sister, was disappointed that Stu hadn't visited their mother even once since her recent heart attack. Bethany, the middle child, was simply furious with him. Stu seemed oblivious to their feelings. He e-mailed them that he had upcoming reserve duty and possible deployment but would visit their mother just as soon as he could.

The sisters knew that, while they had dutifully visited their mother weekly for years, their brother occasionally stopped by. But his behavior now was inexcusable. Bethany confronted him on the phone. Stu shouted back that she didn't understand and had no right to tell him how to run his life.

Clara took a different approach. She asked him to meet her after work to talk. He hesitated but agreed. When they met at a coffeehouse, Clara was careful not to scold him and rouse his defensiveness. She asked him about his work and military responsibilities, and he relaxed while he talked and she listened intently. She made sure he knew that she understood how important his jobs were to him.

When she finally brought up their mother, at first she reassured him that she seemed to be recovering well. Then, Clara asked him quietly what kind of relationships he wanted to have with their mother, and with her and Bethany. Stu seemed taken aback but then answered honestly, "I want close relationships with you. I just get overwhelmed at times." He added, "It is hard for me to see Mom getting older."

Clara said she felt the same. She said that she, Bethany, and Stu, as siblings, knew each other's emotions better than anyone else during their mother's recent health crisis. She said that the three of them could really support one another—and their mother—as other crises eventually occurred. Stu listened. He heard that his involvement was important not just to their mother but to his sisters. He appreciated that Clara was not talking down to him. She believed him when he said with conviction that he would be there for them.

Anger among siblings often arises during caregiving,
making teamwork difficult. By leading with empathy,
we forge new bases for understanding and support.

When Kenny called his father's apartment and, once again, the phone was busy, Kenny knew that it was off the hook.

His angry yelling probably disturbed his neighbors. Once he'd calmed down, he got in his car and drove the twenty minutes to his father's apartment, only to find him peacefully asleep in bed. For Kenny, this had happened too many times.

Kenny hung up his father's phone properly and then drove the twenty minutes home, feeling so frustrated that he didn't know what to do. He was glad that his father was fine, and he knew that he had the option not to drive over there to check on him. But if his father had fallen and had been on the floor all night, Kenny wouldn't have been able to forgive himself.

His father routinely hung up the phone wrong. Kenny had talked to him about it, but it kept happening anyway. He needed to try something else. Kenny decided to buy his father a new phone with larger, lit buttons and an easy-to-see off switch. Then he asked his father's neighbor if she'd be willing to keep a key so that she could check on Kenny's father if needed. When Kenny explained his dilemma, she was glad to help.

Kenny presented his father with the phone as though it were a special gift, carefully showing him how to use it and testing that he did it correctly. Kenny then gratefully gave an extra key to the neighbor. His father never did learn how completely frustrated Kenny was. That was for the best.

Frustration with a caregiving situation can lead to anger or resentment unless we stop and take some time to find creative solutions.

D innertime was fraught with tension.

After Frank's mother died, he and his wife, Jackie, moved into the house of his father, Leonard, to help him out. No matter whether Frank made his culinary specialty, baked lasagna, or his wife made Frank's favorite, short ribs, Leonard always found a way, by scrunching up his nose or suddenly losing his appetite, to complain about the taste of the food. In response, Frank barely contained his temper. Sometimes he stared hard at his dad across the table. He had spent his childhood being the target of his father's unfair critical comments and didn't think he should have to take it now as an adult.

When he vented to Jackie late one night about Leonard's meanness, she brought him up short by asking, "How did your mother deal with him?" He reflected for a moment before saying, "She somehow could see something else in him when he was being tough. She could see that he was sensitive and hurt. She made allowances for him."

The conversation affected Frank. He suddenly realized that Leonard wasn't rejecting the taste of the meals; he was expressing his grief over the loss of his wife and all she did for him. After that, Frank noted when Leonard scrunched up his nose but let it pass. He instead talked about the wonderful dishes his mom had made. In that moment, Leonard looked sad. Frank then responded to him with his own sadness. They were together in that instance, not at odds.

Men often use anger to cover up sadness. Responding to their anger with anger only creates greater misunderstanding. Find a way to meet hostility with greater empathy.

Paula and her mother had always had a rocky relationship.

Paula knew that she herself was opinionated and impatient. She found her mother, Claire, self-absorbed, demanding, and often inflexible. Now that Paula was caring for her mom, running her errands, stopping over every day to make sure Claire took her meds and ate meals, they had more to clash about.

Often, after arguing about her mother's frivolous spending or over-reacting to a critical comment, Paula would leave feeling frustrated and sad. She longed for a warm, caring relationship, rather than one filled with disagreements and debates. Her mother seemed to know just how to trigger her anger, and they'd be off and running again before even realizing what was happening.

The desire for a better relationship made Paula decide to try a different approach. She would try to slow down, take time to react, and stay mindful of her goal. She didn't really want to win an argument; she wanted to have a better relationship.

She tried her new plan on the next visit. When Paula didn't react to Claire's critical comments, their interaction began to shift. They became kinder to each other. Paula realized that Claire had been on the defensive, too. Her mother seemed to want a more positive relationship as much as Paula did. With patience and effort, Paula was able to feel more kindness and warmth between them. Most of the time.

When difficult interactions occur, take the time to slow down and consider what is truly important. Staying mindful of the larger picture helps us to be less reactive in the moment.

C atherine put the plate of carefully prepared chicken, rice, and string beans in front of her mother, Lila, and then sat down across from her.

After a few moments, Catherine noticed that Lila hadn't lifted her fork. "Is something wrong?" Catherine asked.

"I'm just not hungry." Lila looked down at the food as she spoke, not making eye contact.

"You have to eat to keep up your strength," Catherine responded. She had begun to feel a wave of frustration wash over her. She'd spent almost an hour preparing dinner. She had to go home to feed her family next. She didn't have the time or patience for this. "Just try to eat some, anyway."

Lila didn't move. "I can't," she said. They sat in an awkward standoff.

Catherine felt her anger growing. Considering all she did for Lila and the pressures she was under, Catherine felt that her mother should make an effort. Catherine just wanted to throw up her arms and yell. She wanted to take the plate, empty it into the trash, and leave. Instead, she made herself think about the situation from her mother's perspective. She breathed. She waited a moment. She calmed herself down. Then she got a smaller plate, put part of the dinner onto it, and placed that in front of her mother. She wrapped up the rest and put it in the refrigerator. "Eat as much of that as you can, Mom," she said. "You can have the rest for lunch tomorrow. Do your best. I love you." With that, Catherine headed home to her family, as planned.

It always pays to take a moment to consider your options when feeling frustrated or angry. Often, the best outcome results from a clear-headed, compassionate approach.

Bernice knows she shouldn't be so angry at her husband—it upsets her stomach and roils her sleep—but nowadays she can't help it.

His diabetes is ruining his health, and yet he refuses to change his diet. "Doesn't he know what he's doing to himself?" she wonders. "Doesn't he realize the negative effects it will have for me if he goes downhill and needs more care?" Through thirty years of marriage, she's learned that he won't be persuaded to do anything he doesn't want to. But why doesn't he want to take care of himself and, in extension, her?

Whenever Bernice fusses at him for eating sugary foods, he'll bark back at her before defiantly grabbing extra sodas and ice pops. She'll seethe with frustration in defeat. Only then does she begin to shift from anger to a more productive stance. She'll remember the personality of this man she married and still loves—imperfect, hardheaded, terrified of losing control over his life. She likes sitting quietly with him in the living room of their small apartment, watching old movies on TV. He can be gentle and nice after she's cooked him a Southern meal.

She'll also recall her own sense of purpose—to live her moral values, especially helping others who need her care. Encouraging her husband to change his self-destructive behavior is a challenge for her. Venting fury at him would only complicate her goal.

Bernice smiles during those rare periods when she is successful at convincing him to eat better or exercise so he can lose some weight. When he backslides, she feels her anger rising but then tries harder. Though she often feels beleaguered, she fights the good fight through her loving relationship with him.

Feeling angry when our loved ones seem to work against themselves is normal. But expressing that anger doesn't usually improve matters. Developing understanding often does.

CHAPTER 3
Anxiety and Worry

Anxiety is the hand maiden of creativity.
—T. S. Eliot

While caring for our loved ones, it is natural to worry about them. How are they now? How will they be? What terrible thing could happen? Caregivers are regularly challenged to anticipate and plan for crises in addition to the everyday pressures of providing care. Remaining mindful of the present moment can help us to put the feelings of anxiety into perspective. Right in this moment, everything is okay. We can breathe deeply, relax in the here and now, and accept that we cannot plan for everything. We are only human.

We are hardwired to respond more intensely to negative stimuli than to positive.

We react in significant emotional ways to bad experiences, and we remember them better than we do the good ones. When our thoughts become negative, and we focus on what is negative in our lives, we can fall into a pattern of ruminating—repeatedly going over thoughts and feelings. This can have an impact on our health in many ways.

We have the power to shift our perspective. When we practice mindfulness, we are guiding ourselves to stay in the current moment. We experience our life in a nonjudgmental, transitory, and peaceful way. We gain perspective, observing what is happening around us rather than being overwhelmed by it. When we remember to step back, we can let go of the intensely negative feelings and find a neutral state to occupy. Mindfulness requires practice.

Getting to a positive outlook takes effort, too. One way to get there is by remembering to be grateful for all that is good in our lives. Going through a list of good things brings balance and helps us to shift our mood. Making a daily practice of mindfulness and meditation also lowers the intensity of feelings and clears the mind of negative thoughts, allowing us to focus more effectively on positive thoughts. Choosing to do an enjoyable or challenging mind-occupying activity can also help push negative thinking away.

When we mindfully focus on the positive in our lives—moving our attention away from our negative thoughts and the feelings that accompany them—we are truly caring for ourselves.

BARRY:

At 3 a.m. on too many nights, I suddenly awake to racing thoughts, big and small: What did the doctor mean by saying that my mother is in kidney failure?

Does she need me to buy her a quart of milk tomorrow? How can she stay in her apartment if she keeps falling? I roll over again and again, trying to find a more comfortable position and more relaxed frame of mind. But the thoughts keep charging at me from different directions, no matter how much I try to dodge them. I'm awake for an hour before uneasily drifting off. When the alarm loudly rings, I feel as if I haven't slept.

Worry has its benefits. It helps us prepare for the future by anticipating and planning for all possible challenges. But worrying at 3 a.m. doesn't really bring me any closer to solving family caregiving's myriad problems. It only deprives me of the replenishment of deep and uninterrupted sleep, making my brain feel scattered and woozy the next day. There is a word for worrying endlessly, needlessly, and uncontrollably—anxiety.

Anxiety is a problem. It makes us inefficient and ineffective problem solvers. It preoccupies us, causing us to be more emotionally distant from the loved ones we're caring for. Worse, it detracts from our enjoyment of living, often leading to depression.

If I could manage my anxiety ideally, I would regard the 3 a.m. thoughts as merely that—thoughts that have no power other than that which I give them. I'd imagine them as mosquitoes at a picnic, mere nuisances to be slapped aside rather than as marauding beasts capable of harm. I would try to focus on the calming sounds of my own breathing, not the thoughts buzzing. I'd sense the soft bed and warm blankets that surround me, not worry's pinprick.

Anxiety makes caregiving challenging. By recognizing it, we can adopt strategies for managing it while still planning adequately for the future.

Janine tossed and turned at night, thinking about her mother's safety.

She did everything she could think of to keep her safe during the day. She never left the older woman alone, she had safety rails installed in the bathroom, and she encouraged her to wear an alert button around her neck and use her walker at all times. But, at night, Janine worried that her mom would get out of bed and fall. Alzheimer's disease had made it difficult for her to remember to take care of herself. She'd forget the alert button and the walker. Janine tried to sleep, but her own bedroom was right next to her mother's, and she found herself awake, at the ready, in case her mother got out of bed.

Janine realized that this could not continue. She was determined not to put her mother in a facility. She wanted to provide her care. But she needed to sleep at night in her own room. One night when she was feeling especially worried and exhausted, she suddenly remembered that when her daughter was little, they'd used a baby monitor. She had been able to sleep but would awaken if she heard her daughter cry.

After setting up the monitor in her mother's room, Janine was able to sleep better. She still worried about her mother's safety and awoke easily. But she'd found a partial solution, one that allowed her to continue caring for her mother, her first priority.

Finding creative ways to manage our anxiety allows us to continue caring for our loved ones while also caring for ourselves.

When his father, Sid, complained during a phone call that he was having frequent stomach pains, his oldest son reacted strongly.

"Let's get you to your doctor," Bert responded quickly. But Sid protested, saying, "It's just a bellyache." Bert wasn't so easily mollified, however. He insisted that a doctor evaluate his father. Bert got off the phone and immediately called Sid's primary care physician for an appointment.

Later, Bert told his wife, Nancy, about the conversation.

"This is just how it started with Mom," he said, justifying his action. Bert's mother had died two years ago, only a few weeks after a diagnosis of pancreatic cancer. She had had frequent stomach pains for several months, which he hadn't taken seriously. She finally went to the doctor on her own and received the grim news. He was still wracked with guilt that he had failed to heed the warnings promptly and perhaps save—or at least extend—her life.

Nancy listened to her husband with understanding. She knew Bert missed his mother and couldn't bear the thought of losing his father, too. She also knew he was prone to self-blame. "I know you are taking all caution for your father," she said to him. "But the past isn't likely to repeat itself in the future. You're worrying too much that you are going to be responsible for something bad happening."

Bert sighed. He knew his wife was right that his worrying was as much self-protective as protective of Sid. "It's hard," he said. "I don't want to be an alarmist. Thanks for helping me keep things in perspective."

He called his dad and explained his reaction—and the feelings behind them. Together, they decided to keep the appointment.

Past losses often increase our vigilance about potential future tragedies. We may come to worry reflexively. We may need others we trust to point out our exaggerated concerns.

As Doreen tossed and turned, unable to sleep, she could not turn off the repetitive, worried thoughts about her mother, whose breast cancer had returned in full force.

Doreen's partner, Susan, tried to soothe her, but she eventually had to go to sleep in the guest room so she'd be able to get to work the next day. When their two young kids woke up the next morning, Doreen felt so exhausted she wasn't sure she'd be able to care for them through the day. This pattern had become a regular occurrence for the family.

When the doctors found that her mom's breast cancer had recurred, Doreen couldn't help imagining the end, when her mother would be dying in hospice. She thought about it all day long and for most of the night. The terrifying thought made Doreen so sad that she cried frequently. It was hard on the whole family.

Meanwhile, her mother was going for treatments and doing everything she could to fight the cancer. When Doreen visited her one day with the kids, her mother pulled her aside while the kids were eating cookies. "Doreen," she said, "I need you to be strong for me. One day this cancer will probably get the better of me. But in the meanwhile, I need you to be present with me, enjoy our time together, and live your life." Doreen promised to try.

Doreen thought about what her mother had said and talked it over with Susan. Just because she could imagine the end did not mean she should spend her time thinking about it. It certainly wasn't helping at all. With prompts from Susan, Doreen found ways to distract herself from the thoughts; add in other, more positive thoughts; focus on the kids; and make efforts to be more present in her life and with her family. She knew that she'd have to focus on her fears and grief one day, but not before she absolutely had to.

Anxiety prevents us from living in the present and cannot truly
prepare us for loss. If we refuse to allow anxiety to take over,
we can stay in the present moment, holding on to the joy and love
for as long as possible.

CHAPTER 4

Commitment, Intention, and Responsibility

We must be willing to let go of the life we've planned,
so as to have the life that is waiting for us.
—Joseph Campbell

Making a commitment to caregiving—and regularly carrying out that commitment through our intentions, decisions, and actions—has a profound impact on us as caregivers. When we keep our commitment in mind, we find the strength and stamina to carry us through whatever challenges arise. We feel the sense of accomplishment that accompanies responsibility, the confidence that follows from overcoming our fears, and the satisfaction from a job done as well as possible. Our caring commitment helps us grow as people.

BARRY:

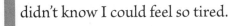 didn't know I could feel so tired.

Not really sleepy but worn, my muscles aching and my mind numb. It wasn't just the wear and tear of providing frequent care—making dinners, picking up prescriptions, visiting regularly—for my mother with mild dementia. It was the sense that I could never fully relax— what caregiving expert Carol Levine has called being "always on call." Even when I was physically apart from my mother, some section of my brain was always mulling over what she might be doing and how she might be doing it and whether or not she was safe.

There's no better balm for fatigue than feeling inspired. I drew on the shining examples around me. There was the older wife I saw in my neighborhood, taking walks each day with her ailing husband. She held his hand tightly and patiently urged him onward. There was the middle-aged daughter I knew who used humor and teasing to keep her cognitively impaired father entertained. There was my mother who, though knowing she no longer had the memory or reasoning skills she once had, still carried herself with dignity and tried her best to think through on her own how to care for herself each day.

Ultimately, I made a promise to myself, as much as to my mother, to help her make a "soft landing" with the hard changes of aging. That conviction provides me with purpose and energy. I shake off fatigue because I know what I must do.

The commitments we make to ourselves and others carry us through times of doubt and depletion. Take pride in your sense of allegiance and responsibility.

The decision to move her mother into her home had filled Gail with trepidation and had taken a long time.

But it was the best solution. Her mother could no longer live alone safely, and Gail was the only person she could rely on. It made sense financially. Still, there was plenty of dread to go around. Her mother knew it had to happen but wasn't happy about it either.

Gail had felt like a disappointment to her mother practically from birth. Gail had been well behaved, received good grades, and grown up to earn a good living in a career she loved. But she had not lived up to her mother's dream for her. She hadn't gotten married or had children. She didn't care much about fashion or decor. Gail and her mother often had little to talk about because their interests were so divergent.

When the time came for her mother to move in, Gail consciously decided to take the time to try to do the right thing. They might never be close, but Gail would make her best effort to provide her mother with a safe, comfortable environment. She'd even try to pay attention to her mother's interests in an effort to improve their connection.

As Gail made that effort, her mother began to as well. The two women gradually got to know and appreciate one another as they never had before. With determined effort from each of them, what had been painful and awkward for years evolved into the precious relationship it always should have been.

When we make a conscious effort to be our best selves and to set aside our differences, we encourage our loved ones to do the same. The reward is lasting, loving relationships.

Maybe her other kids would one day understand.

Maybe they wouldn't. Elizabeth was intent on caring for Willie anyway. He was the third of her five children and had been the bad boy among them practically since birth. When he was a child, he'd relentlessly teased his younger sisters and stole his older brother's baseball cards. Later on, he was in constant trouble with the assistant principal for truancy and with the local police chief for petty vandalism. His siblings never much liked him. They were ashamed of him.

But Willie was her son. Elizabeth loved him as much as any of her other children. When, in his midtwenties, he stopped breathing after mixing pain pills and vodka one night, there was no question she would be there for him. The doctors said he'd suffered an anoxic brain injury. He now thought very slowly and walked with a stiff, swaying, Frankenstein monster–like gait. He could no longer work or care for himself. Elizabeth moved him back in with her.

Her other kids were mad at her. They said Willie did this to himself and didn't deserve all her attention and sacrifices. They complained that she didn't have time anymore for them and their families. These complaints bothered her, and she intentionally carved out time for each of her other children on occasion. But she felt as if she had no choice but to give her best energies to Willie. He had no one but her. She took on this duty when she brought him into this world. She had no words to explain herself—only the demonstration of her love.

The goodness of the world depends on family caregivers who remain committed to their mission regardless of others' judgments. These caregivers deserve our appreciation, gratitude, and support.

When Diane's mother-in-law, Sue, wound up in an acute rehab hospital after another in a series of falls, Diane worried about what to do.

Diane's husband had passed away, but she remained committed to caring for Sue. She knew Sue was extremely eager to return to the apartment she'd called home for the previous eleven years. Still, the older woman's dementia had gradually worsened, and she needed increased support. Diane wanted to help her stay in her apartment but found it difficult to judge how much care Sue would need. She was afraid of providing less than adequate care, but she didn't want to upset Sue with too many aides and wanted to keep the cost down.

While Sue was in rehab, Diane took the opportunity to talk to the nursing staff, the various therapists, and the doctor. Each gave her valuable input about Sue's needs. She spoke to her own family and Sue's extended family as well, asking how much support they could commit to offering. And, of course, she discussed everything with Sue. She took her time considering what she felt she could do for Sue while maintaining her own career and other responsibilities.

Diane devised a plan of care to keep Sue at home with the support of herself, family, and paid providers. She knew that when Sue returned home, they'd have to periodically evaluate how well the plan was working with regard to Sue's safety. The goal was to provide Sue with the best quality of life possible in her home. Diane knew that she'd continue to talk with professionals and family and that the care would change and evolve as Sue's needs changed. Diane was determined to do her best.

When we make the commitment to care for a loved one, we can best sustain our efforts through careful consideration of our own needs over time and with the guidance and support of both professionals and family members.

Everyone was telling Peggy that if she didn't get on a plane and visit her father very soon, she might never see him again.

Her siblings couldn't understand why she hadn't done so already. But whenever Peggy sat down to make her flight arrangements, she was distracted, or tired, or not feeling well. She would then go to bed and sleep poorly because she was actually, she admitted, terrified. She did not feel comfortable telling her siblings that she couldn't bear to see their father dying. He had been her hero, tall, handsome, and strong. She'd always felt protected by him.

Since she'd moved away, she'd visited a couple of times a year. In the last few years, since his cancer diagnosis, she'd dreaded the visits and put them off whenever she could. He had aged so quickly and was now skinny, frail, and in need of the same protection he used to give her. This broke her heart and frightened her. She was ashamed to even think it, but she needed him to be her hero even now. Her siblings would have thought she was crazy if she had told them.

One night while she was having trouble sleeping, Peggy decided to get up and book her flight. She'd see her father in two days. As soon as she had turned off her computer, she felt a huge wave of relief. She realized that no matter how upsetting it would be, she needed to see him. She needed to say goodbye, and she needed to be there for him. She was his daughter and loved him. And she'd have no regrets.

The prospect of our loved ones' illness and death can be frightening. When we remember our commitment to them, we can overcome our fear and do what we need to do.

CHAPTER 5

Community

Grief can take care of itself, but to get the full value of joy you must have somebody to divide it with.
—Mark Twain

Just as we provide care to our loved ones, we sometimes need care to sustain ourselves as well. We are often reluctant to ask for help or even emotional support. We worry that we'll feel disappointed, frustrated, judged, or indebted. What we often overlook is that our need for support or assistance is an opportunity for someone else to be helpful, to experience the reward of giving to us. It is a chance for connection and positive interaction. Our extended family, neighbors, friends, and loved ones all benefit when we reach out for support.

The eight adult siblings sit in a circle on the living room couches and folding chairs with their father in an armchair at one end, listening intently to the lively discussion.

Watching from the dining room are concerned spouses, grandchildren, and friends. At this quarterly family caregiving meeting, the large Kelly clan is reviewing the father's medical condition since his stroke, his current needs for care, and the plan they've together adopted for taking care of him and each other. The meeting, as always, drags on for hours. (These siblings like to debate.) The father's face glows, moved by this show of unity for his benefit and for the evidence of the loving spirit he and his wife engendered in their family.

Few families come together as a working team as the Kellys do. Typically, we foist the bulk of the work on one family member (usually the youngest or oldest daughter, according to research), who becomes the primary caregiver. When stressed by the ongoing care demands, she tends to hunker down and force herself to do all the work rather than reaching out to her reticent siblings. (She contends it's just easier that way because she doesn't want to feel disappointed if they should refuse to help.) Over time, she bears the brunt of caregiving's wear and tear and runs the risk of ultimately feeling alone, resentful, and depleted beyond repair.

What's the best way to create a caregiving team? We have to appeal to long-standing bonds of affection and responsibility. When those bonds seem weak, we have to try to strengthen them by talking directly to potential team members: I am here for our loved one. Please be here for me. I will love you regardless, but I need your help during this hard time to do this good work.

Teamwork matters. To the degree we support each other, we better care for our loved ones and for ourselves. The bonds we strengthen now during caregiving will hold us fast as a family in the years after.

When Marjorie became overwhelmed by caring for her mother, who had Alzheimer's disease, at home, she reluctantly turned to her two sisters to figure out what to do.

The plan had been for Marjorie—the only one of the three who wasn't working at a job outside the home—to provide the care, with the other two sisters providing respite on some weekends. Initially, Marjorie had been eager to care for her mother and had relished the role. But, after two years of increasingly challenging care, she was having trouble sleeping and was feeling anxious; she had to admit that she couldn't do it by herself anymore. She felt like a failure.

Her sisters were supportive and appreciative of all Marjorie had done, understanding that it had become too difficult for her to manage. Although originally they had pledged not to put their mother in a nursing home, all three came to agree that it would be the safest place for her at this point. They visited several well-regarded nursing homes, taking turns staying with their mother while the others toured facilities. All three felt relief after their mother was finally placed in a safe and reputable home, where she was well cared for.

They developed a new plan. Each sister would visit with their mother on a rotating schedule and report back to the others with a quick text message.

Recognize when the caregiving task becomes overwhelming
and turn to caring family and friends and existing resources
to find new solutions.

Anne felt put upon when her daughter, Jane, kept encouraging her to reach out to her neighbors regularly for help.

"You know that I like to do things on my own," Anne, seventy-five, argued with Jane. "Plus," she said, "they're busy people. I want to keep good relations with them by not being a burden to them." Jane insisted that, if Anne wanted to remain in her house with her husband, Jane's stepfather, who had vascular dementia, then she could use all the help she could get.

Anne was determined to minimize the amount of help she received. She had allowed the teenage boys from the family next door to shovel her driveway. She had even accepted a casserole from the middle-aged woman across the street the last time her husband had been hospitalized. But she hoped that these were rare exceptions. When her husband fell one day in the bathroom and she couldn't lift him, though, she faced some difficult questions: Should she call Jane, who lived a half hour's drive away, to help her pick up her stepfather? Should she bother the police or fire departments? Neither seemed like good ideas. Reluctantly, she called her next-door neighbor.

He came promptly. He was a strapping man of forty who lifted her frail husband easily. He made jokes as he did the work as if trying to ease the awkwardness that he guessed Anne was experiencing. She appreciated his strength and sensitivity. Later that afternoon, she dropped off a plate of home-baked butter cookies at his house with a thank-you card.

That began an ongoing arrangement. He and his sons did lifting when needed. She delivered cookies. She also accepted packages delivered when they weren't home. They were better neighbors than ever.

In communities, we have opportunities to both take and give. The bonds thus formed among community members help sustain us through our individual journeys.

Peering through her kitchen window while she did her math homework, Casey, age seventeen, watched the family in their yard across the way.

She knew they had to care for a ten-year-old son who had severe brain damage and three younger children. She saw the father managing the son, while the mother played with the younger children. Just watching them made Casey feel anxious and incredibly sad. She tried to focus on the math she had to hand in at school the next day, but her attention kept drifting to the window.

Casey knew the family but hadn't spent much time with them, although they'd lived there almost two years. She thought about how difficult their lives must be and how they hardly got a break from child care. As she watched them play, she realized that they seemed busy, but not unhappy. She couldn't take her eyes off them, and she was not getting her math homework done.

She got up, went out the back door, and walked outside through her yard toward theirs. The younger children ran and toddled over to see her through the fence. When the mother followed them, Casey introduced herself and offered to play with the kids for an hour. The mother was grateful and gracious. Before Casey knew it, she was running around the neighbor's yard, and the kids were chasing her and laughing. The time flew by.

Afterward, the mother thanked her, and Casey heard herself offer to play with the kids again. She gave the mother her phone number and suggested that if they needed help, they could call her and she would come if she could.

Later that evening, when Casey was trying to attack the math homework once again, she reflected on how glad she felt to have helped out, even that one short hour. She'd definitely do it again.

When we make the effort to help others, we bring them assistance and relief and we bring ourselves joy.

When Denise visited her father, he'd complain about how lonely he was now that Denise's mother had passed away.

Denise spent as much time with him as she could, but she worked full-time and had three young children at home. She'd ask him if he'd called any friends or family. The answer was always no; he was too unhappy to call anyone. At first, people had called him, but he didn't always answer the phone or even call back; some had given up.

Denise decided that each time she visited him, together they'd make at least one call to someone her father cared about. She'd get on another phone, and they'd all chat. Over the months of visits, they called his aunt and uncle, with whom they were both close. They called his sister and brother, who both lived far away. They called a few friends. The calls tended to energize her father. During the remainder of their visits together, his mood would be brighter.

On what turned out to be Denise's last visit to her father before he passed away from a heart attack, they called Denise's brother, David, who lived across the country and wasn't able to visit as frequently as he would have liked. The three had a happy conversation, longer than most, in which their father talked and laughed. When Denise looks back on that day in particular, she feels grateful for that happy, loving time together with her father and brother—and grateful she helped make it happen.

Sometimes our loved ones need help staying connected to their community of friends and family. When we support these meaningful relationships, we bring happiness to everyone involved.

CHAPTER 6

Devotion and Dedication

The world is nothing but a school of love. Our relationships with our husband or wife, with our children and parents, with our friends and relatives are the university in which we are meant to learn what love and devotion truly are.
—Swami Muktananda

Deep, steadfast, selfless care is often as much a blessing for the devoted caregiver as for the loved recipient. When we approach the task of caregiving with devotion, we maintain a larger, more meaningful perspective. The daily chores become only a small part of the value derived from providing care. The rewards of giving our loved ones just what they need stay with us as part of our growing capacity for compassion and love.

While Jordan sat next to his mother in the crowded waiting area at the emergency room, he scrolled through the text messages on his phone and began answering e-mail, making the most of his predicament.

He knew they'd be there late into the night. They had come to the ER because she'd had intense chest pain. The pain had stopped, but they had agreed that she needed to be checked. Neither of them had wanted to wait until morning.

Because he was so focused on his phone, he failed to notice that his mother was quietly crying. When a nurse came over to transfer them to a curtained-off room inside the ER, he was surprised to see her wiping away tears. When they had wheeled her into the little, temporary room and the nurse had left, he asked his mother what was wrong. When his mother just shrugged in response to Jordan's question, he pressed on, "Why are you crying?"

What followed was a long, emotional answer. His mother felt like a burden to him. She knew he had work to do and needed his sleep. She knew that caring for her prevented him from spending time with his girlfriend and his friends. He'd even had to miss work events so that he could care for her. She felt awful that he was carrying so much responsibility and blamed herself. After she spoke, she began to cry again.

Jordan got up and gave her a hug. "It's okay, Mom," he said. "Not only do I not mind caring for you, but it is important to me. I feel like it gives me a chance to give back to you, and I very much want to do that. I love you. Caring for you is part of loving you. You taught me that."

His mother had to smile, even as Jordan picked up his phone to send another e-mail.

Caring for a loved one can be a long journey. Reflecting on the meaning and value of what you are doing makes it easier to maintain dedication to this important task.

When Helene married Jorge, they thought they knew what to expect.

Helene had just had breast cancer surgery and was about to begin radiation. Jorge had been going to physical therapy to strengthen his legs and improve his balance after a stroke. He worked hard at it, as he was eager to care for his new wife by driving her to her numerous doctors' appointments. After many years as a widow, Helene loved Jorge's devotion to her. When she felt up to it, she cooked his favorite foods for him, which he greatly appreciated.

When Jorge was unexpectedly diagnosed with lung cancer, and Helene's diabetes-related kidney disease worsened, they both wondered if they had done each other a disservice by getting married. Each had hoped to care for the other, and now each had developed additional serious medical problems. Both were worried about the future.

One evening, Jorge, practically in tears, approached Helene to ask if she was sorry that they had gotten married now that he wasn't as capable of caring for her as he'd planned. Helene gave him a big hug, and they cried and then laughed together as they both acknowledged that they weren't having the best of luck with regard to their health. Then Helene looked Jorge in the eye and said that she was grateful that they could be there to love one another through sickness and in health. She wouldn't have wanted it any other way.

When we care for our loved one with devotion, and we receive devotion in return, there is no more precious gift.

No apps or social media or frequent phone calls, Gretel knew, could completely bridge the miles from Oregon to New York.

The youngest of three sisters, she had followed her husband, who served in the military, from one base to another across the globe before they had settled outside of Portland. Her older sisters, meanwhile, had never moved far away from their mother's Upstate New York home. Now that their mother was declining due to dementia, her sisters were pitching in to assist her every day. Gretel could only try to help from afar in the role of what's often called a "long-distance caregiver."

Long-distance caregivers, she also knew, are often criticized for not really understanding care recipients' needs and for finding fault with the efforts of those caregivers who are on the scene. Gretel, though, was determined to be a true help and not a hindrance to her sisters. She called often with words of praise for them. Even more important, she asked them frequently about how she could help their mother and them.

Her sisters didn't mince words. They asked Gretel to take over managing their mother's bank accounts and bills; she agreed. They requested money to help pay for home health aides; Gretel sent checks monthly. They wanted her to travel to New York to spend a week at their mother's house to give them respite. Gretel and her husband soon made plans to fly cross-country.

Despite the fact that she was so far away, Gretel did all she could to demonstrate her devotion to her family. Her mother and sisters were grateful. Their degree of communication and cooperation actually made them feel closer to one another than they had in many years.

Not all efforts to help are helpful. Long-distance caregivers best serve the family by inquiring about and then trying to meet the needs of those caregivers who are providing the day-to-day care.

When her seventeen-year-old daughter, Pam, flipped her car in a drunk-driving accident days after her high school graduation, Penny experienced a torrent of emotions, from terror to desperation to anger.

When, after a week in the intensive care unit, it was apparent that Pam would survive but with severe symptoms of a traumatic brain injury, Penny felt sadness but also unshakable determination that she would take care of her daughter.

Growing up, Penny had seen her own mother's determination while caring for her father, who had had a spinal cord injury from a car accident. She had marveled at her mother's steady perseverance not just with him, but with their three growing children. If her mother ever wavered in her devotion to her family, Penny never saw it.

Now, it seemed, it was Penny's turn to be tested. She had no doubt that she would do all she could to take care of her daughter. She was her child. This was her duty. It was not going to be easy to help Pam recover and hopefully regain her independence one day. Penny would walk with her, literally and figuratively, step-by-step for years to come.

Devotion is the bulwark of our caregiving. It translates love into the everyday acts and sacrifices of caring.

Even in his old age, with a more stooped posture and less booming voice, Big Ron could be scary.

His gruff tone still made his four adult children leery of debating with him. His hard stare made his grandchildren squirm when they misbehaved. He wasn't exactly mean, just a fair but blunt guy, forceful in manner.

When Big Ron, now a widower, fell on the linoleum floor in his kitchen, suffering a bad hip fracture requiring surgery, his kids knew that one of them had to move in for a few months until he recovered. His oldest daughter, Wendy, stepped up. She knew her father and his ways. She expected that he would be demanding and difficult. When he groused that he didn't have much appetite for dinner, she patiently cajoled him into a few bites, then watched him devour the plate of food. When he announced that he didn't want to do his physical therapy exercises, she pressed him with quiet persistence until he had to give in. "Grumpy old man," she called him. He called her "damn slave driver."

He wouldn't come out and say it, but he loved their time together. The back-and-forth banter, the toe-to-toe standoffs—he felt enlivened by their interactions. Wendy loved their time together, too. She knew her father was more bark than bite and would work at his recovery harder than anyone. She was willing to parry with him if it made him happier. For all her patience and devotion to him, she didn't expect much in return. Toward the end of his recovery, just before she was to move out, he looked her in the eye and, in an unusually soft tone, said, "Thanks." That spoke volumes to her.

Devoted caregivers expect no prizes or rewards. They adjust to their loved ones' habits and personalities. They persist where others are flustered.

Tori and Toni, identical twins, had always had the sort of love-hate relationship that twins often have.

Toni did a little better in school than Tori. Toni was more outgoing and seemed to have more boyfriends than Tori. Even long after they were both married and had families, Tori secretly held on to her resentment. She'd always had the feeling that despite the fact that they were identical, Toni had something she didn't have.

When Toni developed a fast-growing melanoma that even the most aggressive treatments couldn't contain, Tori fell apart. She felt devastated and couldn't imagine losing the sister she'd long envied and adored. Tori took a leave from work to spend as much time with her as possible. She worked hard to bring the family together to support Toni. She spoke to the medical experts and did her best to learn about experimental treatments. When Toni was finally placed in hospice, Tori was by her side whenever she could be.

After Toni passed away, Tori was bereft for a long time. As she grieved and time passed, she found peace in the knowledge that she'd risen above her old petty resentment and had lovingly devoted herself to her sister's care. She was grateful to have had the chance to show Toni her love and dedication.

When we devote ourselves to the care of our loved ones,
we grow from the experience and we have lasting feelings
of peace and satisfaction from our efforts.

CHAPTER 7

Encourage Your Loved One's Independence

I have not changed; I am still the same girl I was fifty years ago and the same young woman I was in the seventies. I still lust for life, I am still ferociously independent, I still crave justice and I fall madly in love easily.
—Isabel Allende

As caregivers, we often walk a fine line between allowing our loved ones to be as self-sufficient and independent as they can for as long as possible and protecting them to ensure their comfort and security. For our loved ones, maintaining independence can mean the difference between a good quality of life and feelings of helplessness and depression. Yet we worry about what could happen if we don't stay vigilant. Gentle inquiries, loving observation, and periodic check-ins with our loved ones help us to walk that line to our best ability.

Maria, eighty-one, had always prided herself on cooking the meals for big family gatherings.

She'd serve meatballs, pasta, several vegetables, and at least one main dish, not to mention dessert. As the years passed, her daughter, Antonia, had begun to assist her. Before a recent gathering, Maria told Antonia that it was her turn to take over. She was just too tired.

Antonia knew that there was still plenty that her mother could do and that it wasn't really best for her to just give up. But despite her protests, Maria stood firm. She had passed the torch. Antonia could see that there was no point in arguing about it.

At the next family gathering, Antonia asked Maria if she'd serve as kitchen supervisor. Just being in the kitchen, but not feeling so responsible, clearly brightened Maria's mood. She gave direction to Antonia and to her grandchildren, who made the dessert. She tasted the sauces and determined the proper seasonings and cook times. She gave pointers on preparation. When the family sat down to eat, expressing approval of the many dishes, Antonia made it clear that Maria had been the head chef, and that she and her children had been sous chefs. Maria beamed. The family congratulated her on another wonderful meal.

Encouraging our family members to continue to do all they are capable of can help maintain functioning and give them a great sense of accomplishment and joy.

Phil felt frustrated. His father, Lou, seemed to have all but given up since his wife had passed away.

When Lou had married Fay fifteen years earlier, Phil had had his doubts. But he quickly realized what a godsend she was. Fay had been so good to Lou, maybe too good. Now that she was gone, Lou seemed to have trouble doing anything for himself. He seemed inexperienced and resistant.

Phil did not have the time or the inclination to make meals for his father, do his laundry, or run errands. He didn't know exactly what his father was capable of managing on his own, though. After giving the situation some thought, Phil came up with a plan. He'd get his father to help him with tasks, gently stepping back to give Lou an opportunity to do things himself. He'd keep in mind that Lou might need some time to take over the tasks fully. If he absolutely had to, Phil would find someone to come in a few times a week to do what his father left undone.

Phil put his plan into action, having his father drive when they went out, asking him to make a shopping list and shop for meals he'd like to prepare, and pushing him to do his laundry. This way he could observe his father and determine how much help he actually needed. When Lou accomplished tasks on his own, Phil tried to recognize the effort and praise him. Over time, Lou actually grew to enjoy managing for himself in ways he'd never had to before.

Supporting our loved ones' continued independent activities is challenging and can require patience, care, and compassion. But it can result in good feelings all around.

Shortly after Ruby moved into the assisted living facility, her three children became alarmed.

They had learned that she was spending all of her time with Ray, a man who lived several doors from her apartment. Their father had been gone for over a decade, and in all that time, Ruby hadn't shown any interest in dating. Now she was acting like a schoolgirl, holding hands with Ray, eating all her meals with him, and talking about him when he wasn't with her. Ruby's children were embarrassed by her behavior and worried that somehow Ray was taking advantage of her.

They insisted on a meeting with the facility's administrator and social worker. When Ruby's son and two daughters walked into the meeting, anxious with their concern, they were surprised by the smiling, relaxed faces they encountered. The administrator, Susan, who had worked there for more than twenty years, and the social worker, Virginia, who had a decade of experience working with the elderly, did their best to reassure Ruby's family that she was safe and happy. They had seen similar relationships develop many times. Ruby was thriving and claimed to be happier than she had been in years.

By the end of the meeting, Ruby's children, though still cautious, were determined to be more welcoming to Ray and to do their best to accept their mother's new life choices. As the social worker had indicated in their meeting, Ruby could make decisions for herself. That was something to celebrate.

Encouraging our loved ones to make decisions for themselves for as long as possible allows them the most happiness and satisfaction in their lives.

Barbara was intent on pushing her son, Albert—twenty-six and diagnosed with schizophrenia—out of the nest.

Her husband, Doug, was just as determined to keep him home to protect him. They each tended to express their opinions in the strongest possible terms. The result was a tense, divided household. Albert became agitated, and his psychotherapist, Greg, thought the arguments might be exacerbating Albert's symptoms.

Greg met with the family as a mediator and guide. He helped everyone to agree they wanted Albert to become a more self-sufficient adult. The course of action he recommended was a middle path between the positions of each parent. Albert needed ongoing protection, Greg said, but they needed a structured, gradual process to move him toward greater independence. He suggested that Albert first move into a group home with other individuals with schizophrenia. There he would learn living skills to help him gain confidence in caring for himself and his illness. Eventually, as he grew, he would transfer to a supervised apartment setting where he would function mostly on his own.

Barbara and Doug weren't sure whether this kind of system would be right for Albert. But in the spirit of encouraging his independence, they asked him what he wanted to do. He asked Greg some questions about the day-to-day activities in the group home. Then, to his parents' pleasant surprise, he said he was willing to try it. It was the biggest decision they had ever allowed him to make for himself. For him and his parents, this was the beginning of his development into a self-directed person.

Loving parents may have difficulty finding the right balance between pushing a child forward and protecting him or her. We should promote growth with dignity and respect—and safeguards in place.

Receiving the diagnosis of early-stage dementia had changed Terence's life.

Suddenly, he felt that his adult children, Rob and Ellen, were looking at him with distrust. They had already dropped hints that perhaps he should stop driving. When they visited him at his apartment, he noticed that they perused each of his rooms as if inspecting for signs of disarray. They had even left a brochure on his dining room table for an assisted living facility close to Rob's house.

Terence realized his memory was now faulty, and he became slightly confused at times. He also knew his dementia would eventually get worse, making it necessary for him to accept more help. But he believed that just because he had been given a medical diagnosis didn't mean that he was now a hazard to himself. He still wanted to live his life as his own person—dwelling in his own apartment, handling his own affairs—for as long as he could.

He asked his children to meet him at his apartment for lunch. While eating turkey sandwiches and salad that he had prepared, Terence told Rob and Ellen that he understood their concerns for him but asked them politely to not try to take over. "Let me do what I can still do," he said. "If I can't do something, then we will talk about whether or not I need more help."

His children immediately grasped the reasonableness of their father's request. They could empathize with his need to remain in control of his own life to still feel like himself. At the same time, they wanted to keep their father safe.

"I think that talking together like this is the best way for us to figure it out," Rob said. Ellen added, "We love you and don't want to step on your toes any more than we have to." Terence was pleased. They were going to be his partners, not bosses, in maintaining his independence for as long as possible in the face of his progressing disease.

We care for our loved ones when we take the time to determine what they really need. Through close observation, frank conversation, and professional guidance, we can arrive at a balanced approach to helping only as much as is necessary.

CHAPTER 8

Flexibility and Creativity

The difficulty lies not so much in developing new ideas as in escaping from old ones.
—John Maynard Keynes

Caregiving is all about meeting the challenges that arise when we take care of our loved ones. Limitations, changes, and struggles can frustrate us and make us feel helpless. We can become uncertain about what our next step should be, even unsure about whether we can continue to provide the care we so want to provide. Then, we find a creative solution, a flexible way to get past the latest challenge. Not only is the problem solved, but the entire situation has improved. We have strengthened a connection. We find joy in overcoming the challenge.

Nancy had begun to dread the morning routine: getting up and then getting her mom out of bed to use the bathroom, get dressed, take her meds, and eat breakfast.

Each morning felt the same, yet the only end in sight was not one Nancy looked forward to at all. She loved her mother and wanted to care for her.

One ordinary Tuesday morning, in a bit of desperation, Nancy decided to shake things up. Before she woke her mother, she prepared a breakfast of French toast and placed it on a tray with her mother's coffee, orange juice, and meds, all laid out beautifully with a fancy napkin. Then she made another tray for herself. After waking her mother and getting her washed up, she led her back to bed and told her she had a surprise. They sat together having breakfast in bed watching a morning news show. The shared time together and her mother's joy made the extra effort worth it.

Nancy thought about other ways to slightly alter the routine, to make things more fun and interesting for both her mother and herself. One morning, she brought out a crossword puzzle and asked for her mother's assistance during breakfast. On a day her mother had a doctor's appointment, she laid out three outfits, including accessories, to choose from. On another day, they both sang along as Broadway music played during their routine. These changes weren't earth-shattering, but Nancy's misery had vanished. She felt challenged to come up with new ways to engage with her mother and to entertain them both.

Take the time to shake up the routine with small creative changes that bring you and your loved one joy and connection.

Throughout her parenting years, acquaintances would joke about how many kids Josephine had.

"Enough for a full-court basketball game," they'd say. Or they'd quote the old expression, "One mother can take care of ten children, but ten children can't take care of one mother." When Josephine had a stroke and could no longer safely live alone in her own apartment, she found out that her ten children, dispersed over three states, fully intended to step up and keep her in her home.

It took lots of creativity and coordination among them. At first, her youngest daughter, Maria, moved into the spare bedroom of Josephine's apartment for a few months to care for her. But when Maria's husband and teenagers got tired of eating take-out food, Maria went back home and Josephine's oldest son and his wife moved in. When they wanted to take a long-planned trip to Europe, one of Josephine's granddaughters from out of town came to stay for three weeks. Over time, the spare bedroom became like a hotel room, as different family members came and went, each doing their part to provide care to their beloved matriarch.

It was a little chaotic, to be sure. Not everyone had the same approach to showering her or cooking her meals. But Josephine had always liked the chaos of having a large, boisterous family. She found it exciting to see who would show up next. In a way, she got to know them as individuals better under these circumstances than she had when they all lived together years ago as a large group. She loved her family for how devoted and flexible they were. In truth, her life was fuller now than it had been before her stroke.

In caregiving, there are advantages in sheer numbers of family members, so long as everyone's efforts can be coordinated. A spirit of cooperation and flexibility is essential.

Moira prided herself on being a good problem solver, but she had never seen something as tricky as this.

Her husband's Parkinson's disease had entered the stage when medications no longer regulated his movements for very long. Within a day—sometimes within an hour—Finn would go from being rigid to having little control over his muscles to being rigid again. He fell often and hard. She hadn't the strength to lift him.

She hired contractors to retrofit their house with safety features—ramps and grab bars—to reduce the number of falls. Following the doctor's suggestion, she tried giving Finn his medicine in smaller and smaller increments more and more often to try to even out his functioning. When that proved of little help, she created a list of neighborhood volunteers who she could call to help pick him up.

One day, though, on a holiday weekend, Finn fell again and no neighbors were home. Moira felt so frustrated that she almost cried. Instead, she lay down on the floor with Finn and nestled next to him. She began singing the forties ballads that they loved when they had first dated as teenagers. He sang along in a weak, raspy voice. They spent hours talking and singing.

Eventually, she called the fire department. Two stocky firefighters arrived within a half hour and picked him up easily. Finn was hungry and soiled but otherwise unhurt. Moira was stiff from lying on the floor. Later, in bed together, they laughed. Through her ingenuity, a frustrating moment had brought them closer than ever.

Caregiving requires continual creativity and perseverance. We care best when we adapt quickly and flexibly to changing conditions.

JULIA:

When my in-laws moved to an apartment close by so that we could better care for them, we noticed how thin they had become.

My father-in-law's Alzheimer's disease had worsened, and my mother-in-law had become too overwhelmed to manage on her own. They had not been eating well.

I began to cook big meals to share with them on Sunday nights, with plenty of leftovers for the weeks ahead. My father-in-law would give me a hard time about meals, claiming he wasn't hungry and didn't want to eat much. When I let him put food on his own plate at dinner, he'd take very little and stubbornly insist that he didn't want more. And he wasn't interested in taking home the leftovers.

I came up with the idea of serving everyone "restaurant style" instead, placing a plate of food in front of them and jokingly welcoming them to my restaurant. Amazingly, I would watch both of my in-laws practically clean their plates, as the family talked and joked together. In no time, they were both getting healthier and gaining weight. I even discovered that if I asked them to take home leftovers because I'd misjudged and cooked more than we needed, they would agree to do it as a favor to me. I continued to "accidently" cook too much.

Family dinners with my in-laws went from frustrating and stressful to pleasant and enjoyable. I was able to achieve my goal, and they were getting healthier.

When we stay flexible in a warm and loving way, and come up with creative solutions that take our loved ones' limitations into account, everyone benefits.

Jill had always had a huge group of friends.

She'd been popular ever since high school when she'd been voted homecoming queen. Now, at eighty-nine, even though quite a few of her friends were gone, she still received calls practically every day as well as unexpected visits several times a week. Jill absolutely loved it, despite her failing health.

But her daughter, Marcie, was concerned. When Jill wasn't feeling well, she'd perk up for her visitors, and then Marcie would be left to deal with her exhaustion after they left. She wanted her mother to socialize, especially because it meant so much to her, but Marcie didn't want the visits to wear her out.

There had to be a way, Marcie thought, to space out the visits to give Jill some downtime. Marcie wanted a way to communicate with the friends if Jill was having a bad day and needed to rest, or if she had to go to the hospital.

Marcie made a plan: She'd collect the friends' phone numbers and e-mail addresses. Then she'd create an electronic mailing list and send out a sign-up sheet for visits. That way, Jill could have one visitor a day, and she and Marcie would know in advance who it was. Marcie would also e-mail weekly updates about Jill, which could help cut down on the daily calls from friends who were inquiring about her health. The system was not perfect by any means, but it would help. An additional benefit was that the friends could communicate with each other on the e-mail list as well.

Anxiety-provoking situations can often lead to creative solutions, if we take the time to examine the needs and goals. Sometimes unexpected benefits result.

CHAPTER 9

Forgiveness

Forgiveness is the final form of love.
—Reinhold Niebuhr

When we step back emotionally and practice compassion, we gain perspective that allows for forgiveness. We are all only human, flawed and struggling. We can forgive what feels unforgivable when we realize that we benefit from letting go and moving on. We feel lighter, less burdened by intense negative feelings, and freer to strive forward toward the positive. Instead of holding on to old hurts and injustices, we heal and grow.

Crystal couldn't stop thinking about her mother's searing insult.

She'd looked Crystal right in the eye and said, "You're so weak. You let people walk all over you."

Crystal couldn't let the comment go because she knew there was truth in it. She didn't think she was weak, but she hated confrontation. Crystal's mother was surely referring to her relationship with Ty, Crystal's husband, who let her do the lion's share of the household chores. And maybe Crystal's two teenage sons, who couldn't remember to take out the trash or mow the lawn. Or her colleagues, who seemed to call her with a problem every time she had a few days off. Was her mother also referring to herself? She'd certainly been asking a lot of Crystal lately, as she'd begun to struggle to take care of her own responsibilities.

Crystal's mother was a tough cookie; she was proud and didn't take flak from anyone. Was she disappointed in Crystal? What her mother didn't seem to understand was that Crystal loved to bring care and joy to others. She didn't usually mind doing for others, especially her mother. She knew she'd be doing more for her over the coming years.

As Crystal thought about it, she decided that her mother had complicated feelings about needing care. She probably felt badly about burdening Crystal when she knew she had lots of other responsibilities. Maybe she wanted to protect Crystal from feeling resentful. She knew she'd forgive her mother for the insult, not because Crystal was actually weak, but because she knew that her mother loved her. Crystal knew that she could handle whatever was put in her path, including the challenges to come as she continued to care for her mother.

Forgiving others for angry or impulsive words allows us to free up our energy and to empathize with their struggles. There is real strength in the ability to let the feelings go, stay grounded, and move on.

Thoughts for the end of a long, hard day in which you did not maintain your calm, you didn't say things in the best possible way, and you didn't behave entirely admirably:

1. Sit down in a quiet place and breathe in and out slowly, focusing on your breath until you feel calmer.

2. Acknowledge your challenges. Do you feel overburdened by your responsibilities? Are you juggling too many things? Are you drained by the care you are providing? Do you have too little time for yourself? Are you feeling trapped?

3. Imagine that these are the challenges of a dear friend. Imagine supporting your friend with kind, thoughtful words.

4. Now say those words to yourself.

5. Tell yourself that punishing yourself for your imperfections will not make you perfect. You are not perfect and you aren't meant to be. Or put another way: You are perfect the way you are, imperfections and all. Remember that you deserve what others do, too: love, comfort, and understanding. Breathe again, and let those thoughts sink in.

6. Remind yourself that tomorrow is a new day. Ask yourself: How can you make it a better day, for yourself? For your loved ones?

Self-care, compassion, and forgiveness are rejuvenating and motivating. Give them a try.

Take the time to calm down, comfort, and ground yourself
for another day. You are doing the best that you can.
Every day is another opportunity to grow.

Her father, Jerry, was not a nice man.

As Judy was growing up, he was often miserly, mean, and even violent to her and especially to her stepbrother. She knew her dad loved her in his way, but she couldn't open her heart.

As the Alzheimer's disease progressed, he became sweet and docile. When he became unable to care for himself, Judy wanted him to stay in his home with twenty-four-hour care, but her stepmother, still afraid of his temper, sent him to a memory care facility.

The decision was a good one. The staff knew him only as a gentle man and treated him with kindness and respect. Judy's monthly long-distance visits to him, one-on-one, were peaceful and loving. He always knew who she was. She could see the deep recognition and tenderness in his eyes, and he would sometimes even say her name. Once, toward the end, he even said, smiling, "There you are," cobbling together an entire sentence for her. "Love you."

On the morning before he died, Judy asked her stepmother, "How do you forgive someone who has never asked for forgiveness?"

Her stepmother answered, "Why do you need to?"

Feeling that pure essence of love, Judy thought maybe she had already forgiven him. As she held his hand while he passed to a world free of Alzheimer's, his spirit, she knew, was whole.

Forgive if you can. Forget if you can. Talk through your feelings. Write about them. Admit your wrongs. But even if you can do none of that, give yourself a gift: a moment with the pure essence of love.

When her mother, Vera, decided she didn't want any more chemotherapy or radiation to battle her colon cancer, Shanelle, twenty-five, was distraught, but respectful of the decision.

Her mother's three sisters, however, couldn't accept it. Rather than pressuring Vera, though, they kept calling Shanelle, Vera's oldest daughter and primary caregiver, to ask her to persuade Vera to change her mind.

They made Shanelle uncomfortable and angry. She was having a hard enough time coping, without being caught between her mother and her close, strong-minded aunts. If she did as her aunts wanted, she might upset her mother. If she didn't, she worried they'd blame her if her mother died. She kept her resentment to herself and—as delicately as she could—told her aunts no.

As the weeks passed and the calls kept coming, Shanelle's anger gave way to sadness. In her aunts' increasing stridency, she no longer heard blame, but growing desperation and despair. No one in the family wanted to lose Vera. They were all grieving—some fiercely, others silently—and struggling toward acceptance.

In the end, Shanelle forgave her aunts for however much they imposed on her. She realized it was their way of expressing their love. She knew that, when she lost her mother, she'd need her aunts in her life more than ever. She hoped they would forgive her, too, for being the best daughter she knew how to be.

When we understand the unspoken reasons for others' actions,
we may find a way to forgive them. As we gain greater
understanding, our hearts grow.

Karen felt terrible putting her mother, Eleanor, in a nursing home.

But she had to work, and they couldn't afford to bring in paid care-givers. Her mother had no money left except her monthly Social Security, and her dementia had worsened to such an extent that Karen was afraid to leave her home alone. Her two brothers, who both lived at a distance, had argued at first to keep Eleanor in the house. After visiting and observing the situation, and listening to Karen's stories, they agreed that Eleanor needed to be in a nursing home.

At first, Karen was terribly pained to visit. Eleanor would beg relentlessly to come home. Sometimes she seemed completely disoriented and desperate. Other times she seemed depressed, hardly speaking at all. Karen would find food stains on her clothes. The staff people were nice but busy and, Karen felt, not as concerned as she'd like them to be. They felt that after an initial adjustment period, Eleanor had become easy to care for.

On one visit, when Eleanor again begged to come home, Karen broke down. She tried to explain why she'd had to move Eleanor to the nursing home. She acknowledged that she was a disappointment, unable to provide the best care for her mother. She cried helplessly. Eleanor watched her quietly.

When Karen stopped crying, Eleanor said, "There, there, honey. I'm proud of you and I know you do your best." Eleanor gave her a hug. Karen cried again, but with relief this time.

Years later, Karen held on to the moment of forgiveness from her mother as one of her most precious memories.

The warm feelings that we experience with our loved ones are so precious. We hold on to them and cherish them for their comfort and remembered closeness.

Marybeth's mother-in-law, Doris, now eighty-five, frequently told Marybeth that she appreciated the efforts the younger woman made.

Marybeth cooked meals she knew Doris would enjoy. She shopped for her, always thinking of Doris's favorite special treats. She tidied up Doris's home, so Doris would feel comfortable. Doris always thanked her and gave her big smiles.

So it was a complete surprise to Marybeth when Doris's best friend, Trudy, pulled her aside in the grocery story to angrily inform her that Doris was unhappy with her. Doris had complained repeatedly to Trudy about Marybeth's know-it-all attitude, her infantilizing treatment, and her controlling ways. Marybeth thanked Trudy for letting her know, got in her car, and cried for twenty minutes. She felt furious with Doris and helpless about what to do.

That evening, long after Marybeth had pulled herself together, she sat down with Doris and told her what Trudy had said. At first, Doris denied that she'd spoken about Marybeth to Trudy. Then she said that she did sometimes feel that Marybeth was extremely competent, but not a know-it-all. When Marybeth pressed her, Doris admitted that Marybeth wasn't controlling. She apologized but explained that she'd been depressed lately and had a tendency to complain when she was feeling down. She truly did, she said, appreciate all Marybeth did for her.

Marybeth told Doris she accepted her apology, but it took a while longer for her to truly forgive Doris. Marybeth considered the situation and decided that perhaps Doris felt envious of the younger woman's good health and resented the fact that she needed help; maybe putting Marybeth down made her feel better about herself.

Looking at the situation this way, Marybeth could forgive Doris and, in doing so, unburden herself of Doris's issues and let everything go.

When we understand that our loved ones are not perfect and we forgive them for their foibles, we are able to see situations more clearly and are freed from carrying unnecessary hurt and disappointment.

CHAPTER 10

Gratitude

To find gratitude and generosity when you could
reasonably find hurt and resentment will surprise you.
—Henry B. Eyring

A sense of purpose, a feeling of accomplishment, a deeper connection to a loved one—these are the gratifications that caregivers derive, for which they give thanks. When we cherish our moments with our loved ones, we are practicing gratitude. We are opening ourselves up to recognize and appreciate what we have given and what we have gained from our experiences. When we stop and take the time to reflect, we discover that we have much to be grateful for as caregivers.

BARRY:

I sometimes hear caregivers chafe about not getting the thanks they feel they deserve.

Absent siblings and elusive friends trouble them. What perturbs them most is when the person they're caring for simply takes their efforts for granted. They feel it is cruelly unfair that their many sacrifices are trivialized. In fact, it *is* unfair. But there's usually little they or anyone can do to make their loved one express gratitude more openly.

Feeling frustrated at not being valued won't sustain caregiving. Rather, it can breed resentment and hopelessness that corrodes the will to continue providing care.

Other caregivers, though, find a way to approach gratitude from a different perspective, reflecting on how the experiences of caring have enriched their own lives. They say that caregiving teaches them the measure of being a loving family member. They say it proves to them that they can handle adversities they thought beyond their capabilities. They gain a sense of mastery and purpose they never previously possessed.

"I'm thankful that this challenge was put in my life path," says a woman whose father has Alzheimer's disease. "Caring for him is the most important thing I've ever done to make a crucial difference in his life. I would do it again."

Finding personal value in the caregiving experience makes the difference between floundering and thriving in the caregiver role.

BARRY:

No food ever tastes as savory or sweet as immediately after a fast.

No greater appreciation exists for feeling well as after rising from a sickbed. I count myself fortunate for never having experienced the kind of illness or debility for which I would need ongoing care. Even in the acts of lifting my fallen stepfather from the floor or safely guiding my mother up and down a staircase, I've marveled at the power in my arms, the steadiness of my grip. Caregiving gives me a new awareness of my own body. I'm not young but am still blessed with muscles and balance and stamina. When I leave my mother's apartment after helping her get to bed, I skip down the hallway and jog across the parking lot to my car—just because I can.

Providing care for loved ones who themselves were once strong has also taught me that all strength eventually abates. My body, too, will be frail one day. I relish the gift of my health today for the good it can do for others.

Gratitude during caregiving comes in many forms. To revel in your physical abilities to help others is to count yourself blessed.

When Margaret takes care of her father, who has advanced dementia, she looks past the befuddled expression he too often wears to search for signs of the sprightly, silly man he was.

Today, she wants him to sign a communion card for a granddaughter, but not with the formal signature he can still use when signing important documents. "Just write 'Love, Pop Pop,'" she tells him. She has him practice on a piece of scrap paper, and he does it well. He then writes "Love, Pop Pop" in a thin, shaky line on the bottom half of the card. Margaret pats his back, feeling very pleased.

To her surprise, though, he continues writing. She cranes her neck to look over his shoulder. Next to "Pop Pop," he is drawing rudimentary stars to signify kisses. She says aloud to no one in particular, "He's still in there."

This small reminder of his loving personality is a great gift that makes her feel exuberant. She calls as soon as she can to tell her husband and daughters. She later gushes about it to her office mates at work. Her long-lost father was restored for one instant. Brilliant stars in the sky could not have brightened her day more. Those people we cherish may still shine.

Even in caregiving's darkest days, seek reasons to be grateful. Gratitude can boost our morale and sustain us in the face of steady losses.

Like many high school seniors, Vanessa couldn't wait to go away for college.

But she also felt guilty about it. As the oldest of three and the only daughter in her family, she had grown up with special responsibilities to help her mother, Frieda, who had multiple sclerosis (MS), including reading to her when Frieda couldn't focus her vision and vacuuming the house once Frieda no longer could balance to stand upright. Vanessa often felt burdened by these responsibilities and had to admit that going to college meant getting away from them to live the carefree life of most of her peers.

During her first Christmas break home from college, Vanessa gained a different perspective on her mother. She could see more clearly Frieda's difficulties with walking and even speaking, but she also acknowledged some of her strengths. Her mother never complained about or even referred to her increasing challenges. Instead, she gave Vanessa her whole attention, listening raptly and patiently to her college stories. Some of Vanessa's old chores had passed down to her brothers, and she could see that Frieda prompted them gently when it was time to do housework. Her mother, it seemed to her, acted with dignity and fairness, giving her children what she still could and asking them respectfully for what she now needed from them.

Vanessa had had to get some distance in order to become more grateful. Having a mother with MS served as her inspiration to study for a possible nursing or medical career. She could also appreciate how Frieda was demonstrating grace through adversity. Vanessa would try to apply that lesson in her personal life in the years ahead.

What seems like a burden at one point in our lives may be a source of learning and inspiration at another. We are thankful for the lessons we derive from the people we care for.

Everyone always said that, as children, the three Jones sisters—Leeann, LaTanya, and LaDea—were as close as the sounds of their names.

But when their parents, Buster and Denee, needed help as they aged, the sisters became even closer. Leeann and LaTanya talked several times a week to coordinate Buster's many medical appointments. LaDea picked up their parents' bills from Denee and then conferred with her sisters about prioritizing which to pay first. When Buster, lovable but sometimes difficult, protested that he didn't want to take any more medications, his daughters quickly drew together into a formidable and persuasive front against which he stood no chance.

The sisters had heard about caregiving families whose members argued about every decision, creating anger and dissension. The Jones women were all the more grateful for their good working relationships. They talked easily and often. They deferred to each other's judgments about decisions. They prided themselves on their cohesion. Their parents, they knew, benefited from their loving harmony. They also knew that, when their parents were gone, they would still have—and cherish—each other.

Strong family relationships are a great gift. They make caregiving easier and life richer.

JULIA:

After my mother passed away, I'd spend every second or third weekend with my father, giving my brother—who did the vast majority of the care for my father—a break.

I would take my father shopping for food, cook for him for the week ahead, make sure he got a haircut, pick up his dry cleaning. We'd run errands together, stopping for lunch along the way. Sometimes my visit would include a Friday or Monday so that I could take him to a doctor's appointment.

On occasion, my brother would join us for dinner one of the nights I was there. Even though he appreciated the time off I provided him, he also enjoyed spending some time with me, since I lived several hours away. The three of us would pick a nice place and make an occasion of it. My father always enjoyed celebrations. Even when there was nothing in particular to toast, he'd express gratitude that we were together having a nice meal. We always had a good time.

When I reflect on those times years later, even though we were so distraught over the loss of my mother, I can feel grateful. The time with my father, and the opportunity to see my brother more frequently, were a gift that grew out of our loss. The memories of those times together mean the world to me.

When we practice gratitude, we appreciate what we have and find joy in everyday moments.

CHAPTER 11

Grief

> *There is a sacredness in tears. They are not the mark of weakness, but of power. They speak more eloquently than ten thousand tongues. They are the messengers of overwhelming grief, of deep contrition, and of unspeakable love.*
> —Washington Irving

Grief, despite its intense pain, is a gift. It reflects our intense love, longings, and fears about the future. It forces us to face our losses, whether of function or of life. It challenges us to grow in our compassion for others, in wisdom about the meanings of life, and in courage to face whatever lies ahead. We must deal with grief head-on. Embrace and experience it, and deepen your appreciation of life.

JULIA:

My mind can go back to the day my mother passed away so readily that I can almost fool myself into believing that I'm once again standing in the intensive care unit holding her hand.

I can practically hear the machines running and the distant voices of nurses. I can see the curtains, the equipment, the blinking monitors, and the bright lights. I can see my mother's body laid out on the bed, with tubes and wires connecting her to what remained of her life.

She'd had successful heart valve replacement surgery. My siblings and I had been so relieved, even ecstatically happy, for two days afterward. Then she had developed serious complications, and we suddenly lost all hope. Despite doctors' efforts, she was dying. When the time came to disconnect the tubes and wires, we each took a little time alone with her to say a few words. Then we gathered around her bed as her breathing slowed. My sister and I stood across from one another, each holding one of our mother's hands. My brothers were by our sides, with our father at the foot of the bed.

We hugged each other and cried, we spoke about our sadness, and we shared happy memories. Time passed. I could feel my mother's swollen hand grow colder in my own. All I could do was hope that she somehow knew we were all there holding her in our hearts.

Grief can be painful and overwhelming. Having family and friends with whom to share our feelings helps to gradually lessen the pain. If we are blessed with love, then grief is unavoidable.

Even the doctor couldn't disguise the fact that Frieda's prognosis was looking bad.

The lung cancer had spread to her brain, he said. The chemo wasn't doing much but causing her pain. Lauren and her brother, Jon, listened, their hearts aching. They hated to see their mother suffering. They knew it would only get worse. More than anything now, they wanted to make her as comfortable as possible.

The two siblings took a walk on the hospital grounds while their mother slept. They sat down on a bench to let the news sink in. The next step was hospice care, a big step. Lauren looked at Jon and began to cry. Their mother, not yet sixty, was going to die. During the two years since she'd been diagnosed, they had done everything possible to fight the cancer, to gain more time, to help her remain optimistic. They had been optimistic, too, until today.

Jon put his arm around Lauren. That they were losing her seemed impossible, even though they'd expected it all along. After a while, they sat in silence, looking at the trees dropping their colorful, autumn leaves. A breeze blew a bright orange maple leaf onto the bench next to Lauren. She picked it up to look at it. She and Jon would be there for one another, as would their family and friends. She knew that. She also knew that her heart would ache every time she thought of her mother for a long, long time.

Grieving is a long, painful process that requires patience and compassion, both for ourselves and for those grieving around us.

Tajah found it hard to believe that this woman was her mother.

The once sprightly manner had been replaced by a blank face. The once sparkling wit had been replaced by mostly silence. Tajah had loved her mother, Viv, intensely. They had rarely had a cross word between them. Viv was her shining example of strength with grace and sly humor. She still loved her mother, but the woman next to her on the couch resembled her only in physical appearance.

She had learned about this kind of sad, slow transformation from the websites and information booklets she'd read about Alzheimer's. Yet, still—six years after the terrible day her mother was first diagnosed and a few months after the doctors said she was in the disease's late stages—it was hard to fully grasp. She grieved the person her mother was, even as she held her hand, sitting side by side in the nursing home lounge. Tajah grieved as well during the rest of her waking life, while she kept up a cheery look at work or at home with her husband or out to dinner with friends.

In some ways, Tajah's grief had only deepened over the years, as her mother continued to decline. At the same time, her appreciation for who her mother was had deepened as well. She cherished memories of important conversations they'd had, as well as small asides they'd shared. Tajah loved telling stories about her mom to her own teenage children. She kept her mother alive in her mind and in her heart. When she said, "I love you," to the woman next to her on the couch and then squeezed her hand, she meant for now and before and forever after.

When a loved one has a long-progressing disease, anticipatory mourning is normal. Such grief helps prepare us for what's to come and allows us to embrace our memories of what was.

JULIA:

When I heard the sound of the bound books hitting the inside of the dumpster that was parked in front of my parents' house, I knew I'd reached my limit.

For the past several days, we'd been dismantling the home my parents had lived in for more than forty years. My mother had passed away a year earlier, and we'd just helped my father move to an apartment. My siblings and I had gone through everything, each taking more than we could store in our own homes, but not wanting to let go. The shelves full of bound volumes that my father had had in his home office were of no value. We'd called libraries, but no one wanted old, dated, leather-bound books. We only had the dumpster for one more day, so in they went.

I took a break to walk down the long street to the small beach at the end and up to the dock. I sat down and looked around at the water, buoys, a few boats, and the far shore. I'd grown up in this small town, in that house, surrounded by my parents' things. My mother was gone, and my father was seriously ill. I just couldn't bear emptying the house of their things. As I sat near the water, I realized that what I couldn't bear was losing them. It wasn't about their things. Everything had changed and would never be the same again.

When I pulled myself together and headed back to the house, I knew that emptying their house was just a painful chore. The chore forced me to remember the past and face the fact that it was over.

Years later, I still have most of the items I took from the house. When I look at them, I miss my parents and feel sadness, but I also feel the love I still have for them.

Grief is a mixture of sadness and love. Let yourself feel the sadness, although it hurts, and remember that the love will always be there.

When she accepted his marriage proposal, Lindsey knew her husband, Brett, drank too much at times.

They were in their mid twenties, and she thought he'd outgrow his partying ways. The signs were promising. Between his hard work and his ambition, his construction business was expanding. She was sure they'd have a great life together—make money, buy a house, have kids, travel.

But coming home from a softball game one day, Brett, then twenty-nine, was driving drunk and swerved into a tree. His head went through the windshield, causing a traumatic brain injury that, even after months of rehab, left him with slowed thinking, thick speech, and poor balance. He could no longer work in construction and had to sell his business. The dreams that he and Lindsey had were gone.

Lindsey felt angry at him, but also guilty that she hadn't clamped down on him about his drinking years before, though she knew that might not have helped. She also felt terrible sadness seeing him struggle as he walked with two canes or tried to express himself. Mostly she grieved for the future that had once seemed guaranteed. He wouldn't have the larger of their two incomes; she would have to. Buying a house seemed remote. Having kids was now questionable.

She had to let go of the old vision of the future to begin grappling with today's challenges. She forced herself to stop mulling what-ifs. "It is what it is," she said to herself. He could still be silly and make her laugh at times. He was still handsome, if not as agile and graceful as before. He still tried to listen and understand her feelings. She was still committed to being with him. She was ready to start work on a gratifying, if different, future for the two of them.

Saying goodbye to our cherished expectations is necessary to deal with unforeseen change. We should greet the future with a spirit of acceptance and adaptation by creating new, realistic goals.

Brittney was afraid. Her mother's cancer had spread to her liver.

They had done everything they were supposed to, and it had happened anyway. Brittney had always had an extremely close relationship with her mother, Jane, and was afraid that she wouldn't be able to manage without her. She relied on her mother and couldn't fathom going on without her. Brittney frequently found herself crying at night and feeling anxious all day long.

One day, while sitting with Jane, Brittney finally told her about her feelings. As she spoke, Brittney noticed that, despite the fact that she was tearful, her mother smiled at her. When Brittney had finished confessing all her fears, Jane said, "I know you're frightened, Brittney. But I also know that you are brave enough to recognize your fears and to face them. When I'm gone, you'll miss me, but you'll also remember that I'm always with you. You know my opinions and beliefs and feelings about things. You know what I'll say about something before you even ask me. And you will always know that I love and care for you more than anything. That love is inside you. You'll share it with your own children one day."

Months later, when Jane had passed away, Brittney was terribly distraught, but she remembered her mother's words and felt determined to live up to them. She would face her fears directly as much as possible, keep in mind her mother's wisdom, and always approach others with compassion. Brittney's grief was painful, but her mother's guidance helped her through it.

Grief, however intense, can lead us to wisdom, compassion, and strength. In this way, we honor our lost loved ones long after they are gone.

CHAPTER 12
Guilt

Negative emotions like loneliness, envy, and guilt have an important role to play in a happy life; they're big, flashing signs that something needs to change.
—Gretchen Rubin

We are imperfect. We lose our tempers, occasionally put ourselves first, and fail to do what we promised. Accidents happen despite our vigilance. Disappointments occur. We struggle with guilty feelings because the responsibility of caregiving is so important to us. Feelings of guilt are unavoidable when we care for a loved one. The best we can do is focus on the many good efforts we make, forgive ourselves for our mistakes, and continue doing our best.

Whenever Glenda reflects on all the care she's provided to her wheelchair-bound husband, she tends to remember her failures.

He was particularly demanding one day and she yelled at him, loud and long. He rolled away, furious and hurt. She immediately felt awful, horrified that she had added to his suffering, but she was too shaken to bring herself to follow him into the next room to apologize.

After years, she still can't erase the scene from her mind, as if it—and not the car accident that severed his spinal cord—was the root of all her husband's troubles. Among all the loving gestures she has made toward him daily since his injury, this ugly incident stands out in her memory, not as an aberration, but as some telltale sign that she isn't really as good a wife as she pretends.

Why does she feel such guilt? Many frustrated caregivers find themselves yelling at times. If you'd asked Glenda if she ever yelled at her husband before he was injured, she'd say yes, without nearly as much concern. But yelling at someone vulnerable who depends on us for care seems to make us more prone to self-criticism. It's as if we expect ourselves to be perfect caregivers and not just human beings struggling to do the best we can. All we need to do is admit when we're wrong. A heartfelt "I'm sorry," no matter how late, can clear the air. Even if it doesn't, it will make us feel better.

Glenda ought to judge herself on the thousand wonderful things she's done for her husband and not the one instance in which, under duress, she verbally lost her temper. She's so kind to others; she'd do well to be kind to herself.

Guilt adds to our suffering and doesn't make us better caregivers. If we punish ourselves and suffer more, our loved ones gain no benefit. Ease up on yourself and take heart.

BARRY:

Family caregivers have to live with their mistakes, but so, unfortunately, do the loved ones they care for.

When I took my mother to one of her favorite activities—a classical music concert—I was trying to please her. But I decided not to take her walker because it would impede her from moving through the symphony hall's narrow aisles. Instead, she leaned heavily on her old cane and my arm as we made our way to our seats. The concert was excellent, the conductor animated, the string section soaring. But on the way out of the building she slipped from my grip and fell in the street, breaking her tailbone. For weeks afterward, she was laid up and in pain.

My first reaction was contrition: I had taken an unnecessary risk and caused this. My second was anger: How could I have been so stupidly cavalier? My third was determination: I would never let her fall again on my watch.

To my mother, these were overreactions. She had badly wanted to go to the concert and had agreed to use her cane. She was angry at herself for losing her balance, not at me for letting her slip. She thought my efforts to clamp down now on any "dangerous" activity were just choking off her enjoyment of living.

A year later, I still struggle with finding the right balance between risk taking and safeguarding. I try not to compound the crime of leading her to injury with the sin of imprisoning her. We practice cautious prudence nowadays. When we go places, she always uses her walker—and still sometimes falls. When she stays in her apartment and uses her walker, she falls there, too. It rattles her—and me—each time she hits the ground. But my guilt is slowly giving way to a kind of sad acceptance: I have less control over events than I'd thought.

Guilt is based on a belief that we are responsible for what happens. There are times when we caregivers can control what occurs to our loved ones and times when we realistically can't.

Eleanor has not slept well for the past four nights since deciding she can no longer care for her seventy-five-year-old father in her home.

His chronic obstructive pulmonary disease (COPD) has progressed to the point where he needs round-the-clock oxygen. Yet he still suffers occasional shortness of breath during which he gasps, turns blue, and then collapses. She has called the ambulance so many times in the past six months that she can almost hear the sirens in her head and see the frightened looks on the faces of her young children who feared their grandfather was dying. As much as it pains her, she knows he needs more care now than she can provide him.

Her hopes that he would understand her concerns were quickly dashed when she last visited him in the hospital. As soon as she began talking with him about the option of assisted living, he started arguing, but quickly lost his breath again and became quiet. He then turned his head away and wouldn't look at her. She left his room that night in tears.

She feels guilty but is also terrified that he'll die gasping on her living room floor. She wants him to go to a facility where nurses can regularly check on him. Is that so wrong? Will he ever forgive her? He's been known to hold on to anger for months. That would be torment for her.

Eleanor reminds herself that she loves her father and has to do what she knows is right for him and for her family, even if he vehemently disagrees. No matter for how many months he won't talk to or look at her, she'll go to his new home and sit with him. She'll try to make this next phase of his life as comfortable as possible. Even if in a different way and different place, she'll be the very best daughter she can be.

Guilt during caregiving can unsettle us continually. But we still must make our best judgments about what is right for all involved. There are many ways to give care and show love.

Every time Abigail did anything fun lately, she felt guilty.

What right did she have to get her toenails painted turquoise? Should she really have spent the money on that new silver handbag when she already had plenty of handbags? Shouldn't she have brought her lunch to work instead of eating out with her coworkers at the trendy new place?

The reason for the guilt was that Abigail's mother was on an extremely fixed budget. Despite planning and careful spending, her savings had dried up and she was barely managing on her Social Security. This wasn't Abigail's fault, but she felt guilty spending her hard-earned money frivolously, while her mother was forced to be frugal.

Abigail didn't have a huge income, but until recently, she'd felt free to enjoy what little extra money she could set aside. She decided that the only thing to do to reduce the guilt was to take her mother along sometimes. They could get their nails done together, Abigail's treat, now and then. She'd take her out to lunch sometimes, too. Most importantly, Abigail would try to remind herself that she was still entitled to some self-care and fun without her mother along—and without guilt.

It can be difficult to enjoy ourselves when we know that our loved one is struggling. Finding a balance between caring for our loved one and living our own lives is challenging.

When their son Petey was twenty-five years old and social workers talked with them about an opportunity for him to live in a group home with other men with intellectual disabilities, Margie and Brent rejected the suggestion out of hand.

He was their son, they said, and his place was in their home. When Petey was forty and his neurologist made the recommendation more strongly, they still said no, arguing that he would never be comfortable living with strangers and that they didn't think anyone could take care of him as well as they did. In truth, they felt guilty at the very thought of placing him in a residential setting, afraid that he would think they were abandoning him.

But now he was fifty-three years old, and Margie and Brent were in their late seventies. They were caught between two strong feelings now. They still felt guilty when even considering a group home for Petey, but they also worried about who would care for him when they couldn't.

They heard about a program at their county's social services office for aging caregivers of children with intellectual disabilities. A case manager told them that Petey could live in a group home for a month's trial period before they had to make a decision.

With reluctance, trepidation, and, yes, guilt, they arranged for Petey to move into the men's residence for the month. At first, he was confused and upset by the change. But, within a week, he was involved in the daily structured activities at the home and seemed happier. Margie and Brent were greatly relieved.

They made the decision to place their son in the group home with sadness—they really missed him—but also with the conviction that they were doing the right thing to ensure his security. After he had settled in for a few months, he started coming home on weekends. This new arrangement was working. The guilt that had kept Margie and Brent from moving forward with this plan for literally decades had now completely vanished.

Out of a misplaced sense of guilt, we sometimes hold back making decisions that are ultimately good for our loved ones and ourselves.

On a beautiful spring day, George just wanted to ride his motorcycle.

His motorcycle friends were texting him, enticing him to come out. He wrote back that he wasn't feeling well, that his back was bothering him. They teased him about it and continued to ask him to join them. They probably suspected that his back was just fine, and it was. This was not the first time he'd begged off.

George's wife, Carrie, had one of her migraines. She was in bed in the dark, moaning. He felt terrible for her. They'd been to every possible doctor and tried every possible remedy. When Carrie got like this, she needed to be alone in a quiet room. George didn't want to disturb her and he felt that he couldn't leave her, especially to go have fun. So he stayed home and tried to do chores around the house. He felt that was just the way it had to be.

When Carrie finally came out of the bedroom, she saw George sitting at the kitchen table looking glum. Now that her pain was less intense, she asked him how he was doing. She didn't believe him when he said he was fine. She pushed him to tell her what was going on. George admitted that he wanted to go riding but felt guilty leaving her alone. Carrie gave him a hug and let him know how much she appreciated his care. After discussing it further, they agreed that they both needed to communicate better. There were times when Carrie truly needed him to stay home, but there were other times when she'd be glad that he was out having fun, even when she had a migraine.

Guilt can make us reluctant to communicate about our needs with our loved ones. When we do, we can better understand one another's needs and make more informed decisions.

CHAPTER 13

Helplessness

We all have a better guide in ourselves, if we would attend
to it, than any other person can be.
—Jane Austen

Caregivers and loved ones can feel overcome by the difficulties that face them at every turn. Our loved ones often uncomfortably turn to us to compensate for their losses. As caregivers, we rely on aides, medical experts, and the cooperation of our loved ones to get through the day and maintain safety. Disagreements, stubborn resistance, and unexpected events can lead to a frustrating sense of helplessness. Practicing acceptance, patience, and empathy helps us to recognize that despite our feelings, we can forge ahead together as successfully as possible.

Whenever Tanisha heard her husband's key in the door, she braced herself for another one of his bad moods.

Ever since Elvin had started going to his parents' house several times a week to straighten up and do some long-delayed repairs, he often came home drained and irritable. His father resented his help and picked arguments with him. His mother was kinder to him but often complained that he hadn't dusted her living room credenza carefully or trimmed their front yard hedges properly. Elvin wanted to help his parents but was frustrated by their lack of appreciation and cooperation. He thought caregiving would be gratifying, but instead, he felt plain miserable.

Tanisha knew Elvin felt helpless in changing his parents. She, in turn, felt helpless in changing him. When she offered to help him, he refused, stating that his parents were his responsibility and he wasn't going to burden her with them. But, Tanisha thought to herself, dealing with his misery was a different kind of burden to her. She decided to act without waiting for his approval.

She surprised her in-laws one afternoon by cheerfully showing up with a vacuum cleaner, mop, and cleaning supplies. They were glad to see her and chatted happily with her while she had a cup of coffee with them. Tanisha then rolled up her sleeves for the next few hours and scrubbed their kitchen appliances and bathroom fixtures until they gleamed. Then she mopped the kitchen floor and vacuumed the whole house, chasing away dust bunnies and old cobwebs in the rooms' corners. Her in-laws were thrilled.

When she went home and told Elvin what she'd done, at first he felt a little hurt, as if she had shown him up with his parents. Then he realized the generosity of her gesture. He thanked her gratefully. The rigorous house cleaning she had done was very helpful to him. But her caring was the most important help he could get.

Even the most determined caregivers can feel frustrated and helpless at times. Don't wait for their okay to offer them help. Just show up and pitch in.

Geoffrey tried his best to please his mother, but whatever he did wasn't good enough.

She'd let him know that the food wasn't hot enough, or it was too hot, or she didn't like it. He made her bed wrong, took out the wrong clothes for her, and bought the wrong brand items at the grocery store. Whenever he'd go to her apartment, he'd feel so much trepidation that he was sure an anxiety attack was coming on. He'd have to practice deep breathing and tell himself he'd get through it.

One day, while making his mother's bed and again failing to please her, he had a realization. As helpless as he felt to please her, she felt even more helpless needing him to care for her. He decided to ask her advice about the bed, as she sat by watching. At first, she belittled him for not knowing. He waited patiently until she was done and asked again. The second time, she let him know that she preferred to have the bottom and sides tucked in, and the sheet and blanket turned down. He did as she said without comment, although it was no different from what he always did. Later, when he was preparing her lunch, he gave her choices and asked her what she wanted and how she wanted it prepared. When he went food shopping, he made the list with her and wrote down which brands she preferred.

Geoffrey's mother still complained, but when she participated in the decisions about her daily living, she complained much less. Now they could have more pleasant conversations. His apprehension decreased, and he realized that by imagining his mother's experience and coming up with ways to reduce her helpless feelings, he was better able to help her—and himself.

By not taking anger and aggression from our loved ones too personally, we can recognize that they actually feel helpless. Through empathy, we can help them and ourselves to feel less helpless.

BARRY:

The competent family caregiver, I tell myself, is, above all, well organized. But there are days when all well-laid plans break down.

At 10 a.m. on a busy Tuesday, I received a phone call at work from my mother's home health aide, who announced she couldn't come in because of car trouble. Immediately, I panicked. Who would take my mother to her primary care doctor's appointment at 1 p.m.? My schedule was packed with patients and I couldn't easily leave my job. I called the head of the home health-care agency and pled for help. She promised to send a substitute aide to my mother's house by noon. I thought the day was saved.

Later, the substitute aide called me to tell me that she had arrived at 12:45 p.m., too late for them to try to make the medical appointment. And, she told me, my mother was now complaining of a sore throat. Did I know, the aide also asked me, that the kitchen faucet in my mother's apartment had sprung a leak?

For a moment, I felt overwhelmed. Then I shrugged my shoulders and relaxed. I knew family caregiving is an imperfect enterprise and that my mother and I always seemed to muddle through. I couldn't control all that happened, only my reactions to daily changes I couldn't foresee. I'd reschedule the doctor's appointment, call a plumber, and stop by later to give my mother Tylenol. If need be, I'd hire more reliable aides. Perhaps tomorrow would be better; I'd do all within my limited powers to adjust to ever-evolving situations.

No caregiver is truly helpless if he or she can flexibly and creatively solve problems as they arise. That is more crucial for sustainable caregiving than the best intentions or organized plans.

Unlike her two older sisters, Inez had no children, traveled a lot for work, and had more free time, so she wanted to help her parents more.

Her eldest sister, Joan, an attorney, was in charge of everything financial and would be the executor of their parents' wills. Carol cooked, shopped, and cleaned for their parents, despite having three kids and a full-time job. Inez wanted to be there with their father while he was in the hospital, speak to the doctors and nurses, and spend time with their mother while their dad wasn't home.

But her sisters treated her as if she was too fragile. They thought she would become anxious about their father's health or depressed about his prognosis. They worried that she'd lean on their mother for support.

They had it all wrong. She felt inferior and helpless when she couldn't do anything. She wanted to be part of the team. She could handle whatever challenges came up. She didn't want to feel as if she was the only adult child in the family with nothing to contribute, or worse, that they might be worried about her fragility.

So she started to show up at her parents' house and visit her father at the hospital daily. She spoke with the doctors and researched his cancer to learn about treatments, recovery rates, and prognosis. She regularly updated her sisters.

Her sisters continued to visit their parents, too, and do what they did before, but the pressure was off them to get to the hospital or house as frequently.

Her sisters came to appreciate all Inez did and to view her differently. She was no longer the younger sister they had to help parent and protect. She was their equal. They could rely on her. Having a role in her parents' care, as well as improving her relationship with her sisters, meant a lot to Inez. She'd found opportunity for growth in a challenging caregiving situation.

We can feel helpless without a role in the care of our loved ones. Finding our place and growing into it can be beneficial long after the caregiving is over.

When Mary answered the phone, all she heard was sobbing.

It was, she knew, Fiona, her best friend. The two women had been speaking daily for decades, and Mary instantly knew that Fiona had had another difficult day caring for her husband, Bill, who had early-onset dementia. With the diagnosis, all of Fiona's hopes and dreams for the future had vanished instantaneously. Mary had listened many times while Fiona talked through her grief, sadness, anger, and even her love for Bill.

When Fiona was calm enough to speak, she told Mary that Bill had walked out the front door of the house during her five-minute shower that morning. He'd disappeared. She'd dressed quickly, driven around searching for him, and after a half hour, finally called the police. They had found him an hour later, sitting on a neighbor's back patio soaking up the sun. He was fine.

But Fiona was a wreck. She'd spent the hour and half in a panic, imagining many horrific possibilities. Fiona didn't want to frighten him with her feelings, so she'd contained herself until he'd taken a nap later and she'd been able to call Mary. Then everything came pouring out.

Mary listened sympathetically, admiring Fiona once again for her courage and stamina. When Fiona had calmed down completely, she moved on to other subjects. She could ask Mary about her day, and the two women could enjoy a few moments of distraction, humor, and bonding. Both knew how fortunate they were to have such a caring relationship.

When we feel overwhelmed and helpless, finding support
from a caring friend can bring relief and rejuvenation.

CHAPTER 14

Humility

> *The man with insight enough to admit his limitations*
> *comes nearest to perfection.*
> —Johann Wolfgang von Goethe

We feel humility in a moment when artifice drops away. When we truly see the vast beauty around us, the life cycle of birth, death, and renewal, and the ways in which people overcome trauma, pain, and suffering, we feel the humility of our small place in the order of things. In awe, we realize that we are part of a vast, mysterious world. These moments are rare and precious and leave us feeling grateful for the brief window into the wisdom of something greater than ourselves.

Paula loves her husband of forty years and is committed to helping him.

But since he developed Parkinson's disease with mild dementia, she has a tendency, out of fatigue and frustration, to fuss over him at times. "Please sit up straight in your wheelchair," she'll say to him. Or, "Please don't get food on your shirt." She doesn't really want to sound like a scolding mother, but she is sure she knows what's best for him. Still, when she sees the look of hurt in his eyes after she has corrected him, she is angry at herself.

She was recently struck by the difference in her husband's demeanor and posture when their eight- and six-year-old granddaughters visited. The girls came in and immediately ran over to embrace their grandfather. He sat up proudly in his wheelchair, beaming. While Paula was making lunch in the kitchen, she overheard the three of them talking together in the living room. Her husband was more gregarious—telling stories about the family in years past—than she'd heard him in months. Then, during lunch, he ate carefully, without a morsel wasted. It was as if the girls had revived the man he once was before age and illness set in.

When Paula later thought about the afternoon, she felt humbled. Here she was tending to him with strict diligence, but it was the simple love of their granddaughters that brought out the best in him. She realized then she needed to approach him more with her own loving feelings and stop pressing him to do what she thought was right.

We all want to be take-charge, self-assured caregivers. But if
we can maintain some humility, we'll be more open to learn,
adapt, and change.

Several years after she moved into her parents' home to care for them, fifty-four-year-old Elena felt completely sure of herself as a caregiver.

If her father wanted to sleep late and skip his physical exercises, she knew just how to cajole him out of bed and off to the local gym. If her mother had trouble getting dinner organized, Elena would quickly step in to complete and serve the meal. She had the household running like clockwork. Her parents' doctors and neighbors said her parents were much better cared for since she had moved in.

Then an accident occurred that temporarily turned the tables. While carrying a full basket of folded laundry up from the basement, Elena slipped down the staircase and broke her right leg. She could barely walk and couldn't drive for months because of her heavy cast. After taking pride for so long in caring for her parents, she was now chagrined that they had to care for her the best they could.

As excruciating as all this was for Elena, she was also amazed at how her parents managed. They made sure her walker was nearby and brought her pain pills. Her mother could handle light meal preparation, so for several months, the family ate more sandwiches. Her father slept later but also did calisthenics in his bedroom daily and got additional exercise by carrying things for his daughter. To her surprise, her parents seemed happier.

When Elena recovered and was on her feet again, she became a different, humbler caregiver. Because she now had firsthand experience being on the receiving end of care, she was more empathetic toward her parents' feelings when she cared for them. She tried harder now not to take over, but instead let them try to help themselves and even her.

We have a basic human need to help others or we feel like burdens.
The sensitive caregiver creates the means for our loved ones to give back.

When Chuck moved back home to take care of his mother, he assumed that he'd do some food shopping for her, take her to a few doctors' appointments, and maybe even cook a few meals.

He assumed that the move wouldn't affect his Thursday night poker games, his season basketball tickets with his friends, or his weekly evenings playing Quizzo at the bar, not to mention his spontaneous social plans. He assumed that his life would be pretty much the same, with the added benefit of saving on the rent.

When, on his fourth day there, his mother required a trip to the emergency room, he began to wonder whether this arrangement was going to be a little different from the one he thought he'd signed up for. When she required his help managing her medications, finishing a long list of chores, and getting to doctor's appointments during work hours, he felt overwhelmed. When he frequently had to stay home with her and beg out of poker, Quizzo, and time with his friends, he felt resentful. He was in over his head.

With the help of a good friend, Chuck began to change his perspective. He admitted he had had no clue about how challenging caregiving for his mom would be. After a few conversations about how to handle his current situation, he began to develop a sustainable plan. He loved his mother and wanted to care for her.

Chuck hoped to maintain at least some of his previous life activities and a little balance, so he arranged for an aide two evenings a week. To maintain his job and save his leave for when he couldn't avoid using it, he found someone who would be willing to drive his mother to some of her appointments while Chuck was at work. Over time, Chuck developed a newfound appreciation and a sense of humility regarding the challenges of taking care of his mother.

Caring for our loved ones requires flexibility, dedication, and humility. We have to accept that we may have to adjust our own plans or goals to accommodate their needs.

Jennifer's dad, Al, had been married to Marie for only three years when he suffered a debilitating stroke.

Jennifer and her brother, David, were both worried that Marie wouldn't want to be burdened with caring for their father. And they weren't sure how decisions would be made. How much responsibility did they have? They didn't want to step on her toes or appear to take her for granted.

While Al was still in the hospital, they asked to meet with Marie to discuss the situation. Jennifer and David were nervous. Marie hadn't seemed especially eager to act motherly toward them. They were all adults, and she had her own grown children. They had gotten to know each other at visits and holiday dinners, but they all led busy lives and had not spent a lot of time together.

When they arrived at Marie and Al's house, Marie welcomed them with a tight smile. After a few pleasantries, Marie announced that she wanted to be clear. Her plan was to care for Al; he was her husband and she loved him. They had talked about their wishes regarding health care, and she planned to carry out his. She would welcome any efforts on their part to help out, but she didn't want to get into battles with them over decisions. She would do her best to consult them, but ultimately, if Al couldn't speak for himself, she would be in charge. They agreed, gratefully.

Jennifer and David had expected Marie to demand their involvement or, worse, indicate that she wanted to leave the marriage, knowing that Al would probably be disabled for the rest of his life. Instead, Marie had impressed them with her commitment and care. They left that meeting awed by her integrity, questioning whether they would have been capable of making the same decision in the same circumstance. Both were determined to help out as much as they were able.

When we witness true commitment and devotion in another, we feel a sense of humility and awe. The impressive behavior of others can be an inspiration and guide for us.

When she used to visit her parents' house every day to help care for her father who suffered from dementia, Lucille was always awed by her mother's performance.

A short, slight woman with a quiet voice, Estelle was kind but firm, loving but determined—the classic iron fist in a velvet glove. Better than any professional aide or other family member, she could calm her husband down with a stern word when he was agitated and motivate him with an imploring look when he was resistant. Because she was so intent on keeping him at home with her, she never tired or complained about her caregiving duties.

Then Estelle died in her sleep of a sudden heart attack, and the family was thrown into an uproar. After a hurriedly called meeting, the adult children and other relatives decided that Lucille and her husband would move into her parents' home to care for her father. Lucille was daunted by the task of living up to her mother's caregiving example.

Lucille humbly approached her new duties, aware she would never have Estelle's commanding presence. But memories of her mother— the looks, tone, and determination—guided her. She emulated the kind but firm approach, and her father mostly responded well. She even brought out old photo albums and phonograph records at times, the way her mother had, to stimulate her father's recall.

Lucille felt as if she was walking in the footsteps Estelle had made along the caregiving path. She sometimes had a sense that her mother was present and walking silently with her. In caring for her father each day in this way, she was cherishing both of her parents.

In the sacrifices we make and the work we do to care for loved ones, we serve as testament to the inspiring examples set by caregiving family members who came before us.

CHAPTER 15

Humor

Laughter and tears are both responses to frustration and exhaustion. I myself prefer to laugh, since there is less cleaning up to do afterward.
—Kurt Vonnegut

Sharing a smile and a happy laugh brings us emotionally closer to our loved ones. When we find something we can laugh about together, we simultaneously step back from our negative feelings and step closer to one another. The warm feelings, the sense of connection, and the momentary letting go of our burdens are a breath of fresh air when we most need it. The world feels brighter and easier to manage. Despite our daily challenges, we feel relieved, renewed, and reenergized when we share humor.

JULIA:

My father and I sat across from each other having an early-bird dinner in the nearly empty sushi restaurant near his apartment.

My brother and I had recently convinced him to move there; we'd been concerned about his health problems and felt he needed to live closer to my brother and in an apartment on one level. My mother had passed away unexpectedly a year earlier, and my father had not been managing well living alone in the big old house they'd shared for more than forty years; its every corner reminded him of her. Since her death, he and I had cried together at their kitchen table on many occasions. Now, he longed for a fresh start in a new place. He hoped that he'd feel less sad and lonely. I hoped we could connect around something other than our grief, although that had been extremely meaningful. For most of my life, my father had worked long hours and had been remote.

Here, over sushi and colorful drinks, I found myself telling him amusing stories about my children and watching him laugh. The joy I felt at being able to make him smile and laugh is one of my fondest memories since he passed away a few years ago.

Connecting over stories and sharing humor is a relief from the sadness and struggle of so many caregiving situations. Finding the levity in the world around you can bring priceless moments of happiness.

Take the opportunity to notice the humor in life
and share a laugh with those we care for.

After Annmarie's father had passed away, she'd find her mother, Lola, sitting in her chair staring off into space.

Since losing her husband, Lola's natural tendency toward depression had worsened. Annmarie's father had always brought humor and liveliness to their marriage, family, and just about everywhere else. Dinners with only Annmarie and her mom had gotten quiet. Annmarie wasn't naturally funny and felt she could never fill her father's shoes in that regard.

Then one day Annmarie turned on the television for her mother and an old funny movie happened to be on. They both laughed. The mood in the house lightened. Annmarie had an idea. Every day, they'd find something funny to watch together and get in a good laugh. Annmarie could never replace her father, but she and her mother could enjoy humor together again.

Enjoying humor together is like a breath of fresh air,
bringing relief, comfort, and connection.

Marvela and her daughter, Philomena, found themselves having the worst day.

The plan had been simple: go out to lunch a few blocks away. Just as they were about to get in the car, Philomena noticed that the back of Marvela's slacks were wet. She took Marvela gently by the arm and walked her back to the apartment to change her clothes.

The second time out to the car was fine until Philomena asked Marvela to see if she had her credit card in her purse. Marvela didn't have her eyeglasses and couldn't find her bank card. Back into the apartment they went to find the glasses and the credit card. They found the glasses on the kitchen table and then found the card in the purse after all.

The third time out, they made it to the diner and were sitting at the table when Philomena noticed that Marvela wasn't wearing her hearing aids. She couldn't hear a thing the waitress said. They managed to order her favorite split pea soup anyway. It was delicious, except that a big spoonful wound up on the front of Marvela's new white blouse. When Philomena pointed it out and Marvela looked down, Philomena thought her mother might start to cry from frustration. Instead, after a moment of disbelief, Marvela began to laugh. "I'm a mess, aren't I?" she said. Philomena began to laugh, too. They joked about what else could possibly go wrong. Whatever it was, they were ready for it.

Maintaining a sense of humor in the face of frustration helps us to keep perspective and feel able to handle whatever comes our way.

Even though Loralie had two brothers, she was the only one who thought to clean out their eighty-nine-year-old father's refrigerator when she visited him every couple of months.

Frequently, it would hold frightening and nauseating surprises. She'd find the usual suspects: tinfoil-wrapped unidentifiable leftovers, baggies of something green, moldy bread. Loralie could manage those. What made her want to scream and run out of the house was the asparagus.

Loralie's father was doing pretty well for his age, managing mostly on his own and preparing his own meals. A friend drove him to the supermarket for weekly shopping trips. He was beginning to have a tendency to forget and repeat himself. Every time he went to the supermarket, he would buy asparagus and put it in the vegetable drawer in the refrigerator. But he would forget to cook it. When Loralie visited, she'd find the drawer full of asparagus mush and greenish liquid, with an overpowering smell of decay. Each time, while gagging, she'd force herself to throw out the contents and clean out the drawer. Then she'd mention to her father that a lot of asparagus had gone bad in the fridge. He would thank her for cleaning it out, admitting that he never bothered to do it.

When, later in the day, she took him to the supermarket, he headed right over to the asparagus section and selected a nice bunch to put in the shopping cart. Loralie stared at him in disbelief. He looked at her with a smile and said that he enjoyed asparagus and would be making it later in the week. Loralie just had to laugh. She knew what she'd find in the vegetable drawer on her next visit.

Sometimes when a ridiculous problem is impossible to solve, we just see the absurdity in it and have a good laugh.

Paola's father, Juan, seventy-eight, struggled to remember what he'd eaten for breakfast, whether it was Paola or her sister-in-law who had visited him on any given day, and even what day it was.

To Paola, his youngest child, Juan had always been full of wisdom and humor. She'd had tremendous admiration for him her entire life. She felt so sad watching him decline, and she knew that she was losing him. When she visited him at the assisted living facility, she'd look at him sadly, and he'd look sadly back at her. Paola wanted to get as much time as possible with him, even though each visit felt sad.

One day, she stopped by to see him with her sister-in-law, who walked into his apartment smiling and laughing. He immediately smiled back. She made a silly face at him and he laughed. She made a simple joke and he laughed again. Paola was astonished. Right in that moment, she realized that her father's mood could change easily because his short-term memory was failing. Paola took his hands, smiled at him, and told him she loved him more than the earth and sky. He smiled warmly back at her and told her he loved her, too.

Paola's sister-in-law put her arms around them both and said, "We are one big, happy, loving family! How did we get so lucky?" For Paola, the realization that she could bring humor and happiness to her father, despite his sad circumstances, was a priceless gift. She'd save her sad feelings for when she was away from him and make the most of their time together.

Sharing humor with our loved ones eases the pain of loss and grief and gives us joy in the remaining moments together.

CHAPTER 16

Joy and Happiness

If you want others to be happy, practice compassion.
If you want to be happy, practice compassion.
—The Dalai Lama

Moments of joy like laughing deeply with a loved one, looking at the bright blue sky on a sunny day, and receiving a child's happy embrace bring us relief from pain and make life worth living. There is so much pain in the human condition. We age, suffer, and lose those we love. We must mindfully seek out joyful experiences, create them where we can, and appreciate them to the fullest when we encounter them.

When Francine's friends would ask her how she was holding up, she'd report that she was just fine, and they would look surprised.

They knew that she'd been caring for her mother for more than five years, mostly by herself. They knew that her mother had Alzheimer's disease and could no longer speak. She also had symptoms of Parkinson's disease that made her movements difficult. Most of her friends couldn't imagine being just fine, caring for someone with such intense needs. But Francine always seemed to have a smile on her face.

What they didn't understand fully was that Francine adored her mother and enjoyed taking care of her. The two had always been extremely close. Francine worried about what would happen once her mother was gone. That worry made her appreciate every day they had together. Of course, there were challenging days and moments when Francine could have used some help. But these were balanced with the knowledge that she was providing loving care for her mother.

Francine wasn't without sadness and pain. She'd had losses in her life, failed relationships, and struggles with jobs. She knew that she was slowly losing her mother, the most important person in her life. But she focused on the joy of caregiving and her ability to provide loving care for her mother, who had become helpless. It would be the most important and joyful effort of her life.

When we focus on the joy we feel providing care for our loved one, the struggles fade in importance and our love rises to the forefront of our experience.

Louis hugged Suzy and smoothed her hair. He adored his wife, but he was worried.

They had just gotten home from the doctor's office, where they had learned that Suzy had a moderate degree of dementia. Louis didn't know what that meant exactly, although the doctor had explained it. All he knew was that he loved his wife of fifty-two years and planned to care for her to the best of his ability. He'd already been doing that for fifty-two years. He had known how to do that so far, but it seemed that the rules had now changed. Louis needed to adjust. He wanted to do it right.

Suzy had become forgetful, was having difficulty finding words, and would sometimes become disoriented. Rather than focus on what wasn't working, though, Louis planned to spend time with her focusing on the clear memories she did have. They'd raised their children, traveled, and enjoyed so much time together sharing both adventures and relaxation. They had plenty to talk about. She'd been such a support to him; he'd be her guide now, making sure she was as calm and comfortable as possible.

Their marriage was shifting, but their love for one another held strong. Louis planned to find the joy in life every day and to remember to appreciate what he had. Everything would be okay.

Remember to appreciate what you have and to find the joy in your relationships with those you love and in life's everyday activities.

JULIA:

My father-in-law, Steve, was still able to walk, despite symptoms of Parkinson's disease, when we decided to go apple picking.

Because his Alzheimer's disease was worsening, my in-laws had moved from Florida several months earlier. They hadn't picked apples in years. My teenage son and my in-laws piled into my car for the short drive. We carried the fold-up soccer chair out to the orchard, and my son helped his grandfather walk on the uneven ground.

The walk was long for Steve, and he complained loudly about it. We were all afraid we'd made a terrible mistake dragging him with us, although we couldn't have left him home alone. Steve managed to sit in the soccer chair at the edge of the orchard at the top of the hill so that he could watch us picking. Once he was sitting, he relaxed. He watched his wife, daughter-in-law, and grandson fill two large baskets with apples. The sun shone and the breeze blew. A big smile grew on his face.

While we took the long, slow walk back from the orchard to the car, we talked about what we were planning to do with all the apples. I'd bake apple pies, and my mother-in-law would make applesauce. The mood was happy and everyone had enjoyed the outing.

Steve's health declined rapidly after that. He passed away within three years of their move. His wife, my mother-in-law, is now in declining health herself. But the joyful, sunshiny memories from that day of apple picking can still bring a smile to her face.

When we come together as a family for an enjoyable activity, we create lasting happy memories.

When Gregory visited his dad, Joe, he'd often feel as if he was on auto-pilot.

Several times a week, he'd check in to see if Joe needed any groceries, medications, or help with anything. Often, he'd find him watching television. As Gregory moved through the apartment, Joe would barely acknowledge him. Sometimes all he'd get was a nod.

Joe hadn't been an affectionate dad; he'd never shown much interest in Gregory, leaving most of the child rearing to his now deceased wife. Gregory missed his mother, who had always brokered the relationship between father and son. He often thought about how he and his father were alone in their separate worlds, neither one with much practice in reaching out to the other.

One day, Gregory decided to take a lesson from his mother. She didn't wait for some other person to set the mood; she brought joy with her. On his next visit, Gregory sat down with his father and reminded him of the time the three of them had vacationed at Niagara Falls. Joe responded with his own memories. When Gregory went home that night, he felt his own mood had lifted, and he knew his father felt better, too.

When we mindfully bring a happy mood and make an effort to engage, we can brighten loved ones' days and help them to experience more joy.

Every week for the past year, John drove reluctantly to the plain brick nursing home where his father, Sal, had moved after his stroke.

He loved his father and wanted to see him. But the spare, antiseptic facility lacked the warmth of the tidy house where Sal had happily spent his retirement years. The previously laid-back Sal had changed. The stroke had left him half paralyzed and wheelchair bound, along with a fluctuating but mostly morose mood. He'd be angry one moment, crying the next, and then suddenly have a sour look. John found it unsettling.

On a Sunday afternoon when John was babysitting his daughter's rambunctious four- and five-year-old sons, he decided to take them to the nursing home to visit Sal. As soon as the boys saw Sal asleep in the hallway, they ran toward him and jumped in Sal's lap before John could stop them. Sal yelled in surprise, but the boys paid no attention. They remembered nothing of what their great-grandfather was like before or where he used to live; they loved him as he was, in this interesting place. After John shooed them off Sal's lap, they each grabbed a handle at the back of the wheelchair and started pushing Sal down the hall, while John trailed behind them.

For the next hour, the boys pushed Sal up and down every corridor in the building, veering into walls occasionally and once nearly colliding with another wheelchair. To John's surprise, Sal seemed elated, smiling broadly and laughing each time they went around a corner too fast. John laughed, too, to see his father and grandchildren having so much fun. It was a sign that joy was possible even after disability and a reminder that children—without adults' preconceptions of how a loved one should be—were able to create joy with anyone in any place.

We make our own joy by embracing all opportunities for fun.
Focus less on what's been lost and more on what's still possible.

All their lives, Aileen and Camille had heard stories about their father's adventures in the wild.

Drew had hiked the Appalachian Trail in his twenties. He'd camped out in the Grand Canyon. He had even hitchhiked across the country. Even after he'd settled down, married, and had his two daughters, he took them camping, taught them survival skills, and told them scary stories around the campfire.

After the girls left home, Drew and his wife had gotten a recreational vehicle and driven to national parks whenever they had vacation time. After they retired, they spent even more time on the road, until at age eighty, the girls' mother passed away. Then Drew's diabetes led to several toe amputations and the need for a wheelchair. Aileen and Camille worried that Drew had become depressed.

They did some research and found a park with paved paths that wasn't too far away. They packed a picnic lunch and told Drew he was going on an adventure. He immediately perked up. After spending a beautiful day walking and wheeling in the park, having lunch at a scenic spot, and letting Drew tell them about the birds, trees, and flowers, the girls took him home. He looked happier than he had in a long time. He gave Aileen and Camille big hugs. They planned to take him out as often as they could.

Despite painful circumstances, we can find happiness in the time we spend together in activities we enjoy.

CHAPTER 17
Know Your Limits

Once we accept our limits, we go beyond them.
—Albert Einstein

As caregivers, we do all we can to meet the needs of those we love. However, expecting perfection, refusing assistance, and pushing ourselves can lead to disappointment and frustration. We provide the best care for our loved ones and for ourselves when we take the time to evaluate the limits of our capabilities. We might have to change our plans, ask for help, or find a compromise. Knowing, communicating, and accepting our limits, so that we find flexible solutions to problems that arise, allows us to continue to provide for loved ones over time.

The first time Edward stayed with Aunt Nancy by himself, he was definitely in over his head.

He had offered to give his cousin and her husband—Nancy's daughter and son-in-law—the weekend away. They were taking care of Nancy with no help, and it was their wedding anniversary. Nancy had always been Edward's favorite aunt, and he'd been looking forward to spending time with her.

In the evening, after he had made a nice dinner and cleaned up, Nancy asked him to help her shower and change into pajamas. Edward was nervous. He'd never before helped anyone to shower, and this was his aunt. He mumbled his reluctance, but since Nancy didn't hear him, she readied herself, expecting his assistance. He did not feel equipped to help her shower, nor did he feel comfortable with this level of intimacy with his aunt. He spoke up more loudly. Nancy finally heard him and agreed that it would be safer and more comfortable for them both if they skipped that evening's shower.

When the weekend was over, Edward discussed what had happened with his cousin and her husband. They understood his reluctance to help Nancy shower. More than ever, Edward appreciated all that his cousin and her husband were doing, and he promised himself that he would offer to help them more often.

Even when care seems daunting, if we communicate and set limits where necessary, we can help out and feel good about what we are doing for our loved ones.

I n the late afternoon, Brandi puts her energies and organizational skills to the test.

Rushing out of the high school where she works in the cafeteria, she swings by the corner where Ivan, her twelve-year-old son, is just disembarking from the school bus. She quickly takes him home, gives him a healthy snack, and then races him to his soccer practice. Then she makes a pharmacy run for her aging mother's prescriptions and a trip to the supermarket to buy pork chops for tonight's dinner. She picks up Ivan, drops off meds at her mother's, prepares dinner, cleans up, and helps Ivan with his homework. Next she goes back to her mother's apartment to help her prepare for bed and then goes home again to reheat dinner for her husband, who worked late. When he mentions that she forgot to pick up his dry cleaning—which she'd promised to do since it was next door to the supermarket—she doesn't know whether to yell at him or cry. She is exhausted.

Brandi loves her family members and wants to help them all. But she is doing so many things for so many loved ones that she feels constant guilt that she isn't doing a good job at anything for anyone. She doesn't know how to change the situation without letting everyone down.

When she calls her mother that night, she cries. Her mother listens quietly as Brandi vents about how overwhelmed she feels. Then her mother says, "We are all so appreciative for what you do for us. But your husband, son, and I don't expect perfection. Just knowing you care and that you try your best is enough." Brandi cries a little harder, but now with some relief.

Her mother goes on to suggest that she hire someone to drive her to the supermarket and pharmacy. Her daughter protests at first but gives in when her mother says that Brandi should focus on her own family first. Brandi is grateful her mother has given her permission to prioritize and make her life more manageable.

If we aim for perfection in our caregiving, we will be wracked with disappointment and guilt. Our loved ones need good enough caregivers. With humility and planning, we can manage that.

BARRY AND JULIA:

We arrived at Barry's mother's apartment to take her to the movies.

She'd been eagerly mentioning it on the phone for several days, insisting that she felt up to it. Although her health fluctuated, she'd been doing pretty well. We were planning to go.

When we walked in the door, we knew something wasn't right. She looked great, from her coordinated outfit to her proper makeup. Clearly, the aide had helped her prepare for her outing. She was sitting in her chair, purse in her lap, smiling. But her eyes looked a little glassy, and when she got up, even with the help of her walker, she had terrible balance and looked as if she could fall down at any time.

Because we'd seen it before, we suspected that she had another urinary tract infection. We asked her about symptoms, and she reluctantly admitted to having them. Barry called her doctor for a prescription and appointment. Then we asked her what she thought we should do. She sighed and said, "I guess I should stay home."

We helped her change into her nightgown, washed off the makeup, and helped her to bed, promising a rain check. We found a movie on television, brought in a bowl of pretzels, and all sat on the bed to watch until she fell asleep. We felt sad but relieved that she had made the right decision.

Making a decision to limit an activity can be difficult, especially when we are disappointed by that choice. Remaining as flexible as possible allows us to choose the safest option.

Ruth thought she had a perfect plan for her growing family.

She and her husband, Jeff, and their two young daughters would grate-fully accept her mother Elisa's invitation to live in her big old house so they could save money for a house of their own. Elisa would help take care of her daughters while Ruth and Jeff were at work. On weekends, the younger couple would do the physical chores around the house that were now too difficult for Elisa.

None of them foresaw that, after two years of living under the same roof, Elisa would have a stroke that left her with right-sided weakness and a limp. Ruth was suddenly in a terrible bind. While still at the hospital, Elisa began pressuring her to commit to continue living with her; she felt entitled to Ruth's ongoing support. Jeff, meanwhile, was hinting that he wanted Ruth and the girls to move out soon; he was afraid that they might be stuck staying with Elisa indefinitely.

Ruth knew her conscience, but also her limitations. She couldn't very well abandon her mother; moving was off the table for now. But she also couldn't neglect the needs of her husband and children by throwing herself into caring for Elisa, no matter how entitled her mother felt. She would have to strike a compromise: They would stay in the house, but Ruth would insist that her mother hire home health aides to handle many of the caregiving tasks.

Neither Elisa nor Jeff was likely to be pleased with this compromise. But Ruth knew she wasn't capable of meeting all their needs in exactly the ways they wanted. She would do the best she could to help every-one involved. She felt sure they would do the same.

We bear responsibilities for multiple family roles. By knowing the limits of our energies and capabilities, we are better able to find compromises to please others and ourselves the best we can.

BARRY:

I hadn't intended to irritate the nursing supervisor, but in my efforts to advocate for my stepfather, Steve, in the dementia unit where he spent the last two years of his life, I wound up criticizing his nursing care.

The supervisor glared at me and responded in a curt, firm tone. I had accomplished little more than to make her defensive.

This occurred, in part, because I overstepped the limits of my understanding. I had spent more than twenty years as a psychologist working in medical settings and thought myself something of an authority on dementia, medications, and the workings of health-care facilities. But, in short order, the supervisor pointed out holes in my knowledge and reasoning.

It also occurred, in part, because of the limits of my empathy for the staff. I was so preoccupied with worries about Steve's deteriorating condition that I wasn't listening well to his nurses' explanations. I could only see problems, not perceive that the staff members were doing their best in bad circumstances. My frustrations only frustrated them.

When I got nowhere with the supervisor, I had to reconsider what I did and did not know. I realized that I didn't grasp all the factors affecting Steve's care and couldn't help him if I alienated his professional caregivers. I learned.

The next time I arrived at the nursing home, I made sure to ask the nurses' perspectives on how Steve was doing. I listened, commented on what they seemed to be doing right for him, and then commiserated with them about the distressing symptoms that couldn't be changed.

We got along better after that. They knew I wasn't interested in judging them so much as supporting their efforts to care for Steve.

I knew I was on more solid ground by being a concerned family member who was respectful of my own strengths and limitations —and theirs.

Being too sure of what we know may close us off to the insights of others. Appreciate what you know; savor the contributions that others may have to offer.

J ared put his arms around Ivan, bending awkwardly down to his wheelchair.

He would try to do whatever Ivan needed for as long as he needed it. Ivan smiled. He appreciated Jared's devotion. They'd been together for more than twenty years. Ivan had cared for him lovingly when he'd gone through a serious depression a decade earlier. Since then, Jared's health had improved, but Ivan's had worsened. It was Jared's turn to do the caregiving, and he was eager to show his dedication.

Ivan's Parkinson's disease had become worse. He needed the wheelchair all the time now. Bathing him had gotten difficult. They still took walks—taking walks had always been an activity that the two men had enjoyed together, and Jared wanted them to continue to get out to enjoy nature. Ivan had always been the better cook, but Jared did his best with guidance from Ivan. As the challenges of caregiving increased, Jared knew that he needed some support so that he could continue doing as much as possible.

He brought in aides to help with bathing and with transferring Ivan to and from the wheelchair. At first, Ivan protested; he didn't want strangers taking care of him. But when Jared explained that he wanted to avoid injuring himself, and that he needed to do some self-care to continue to do all he did, Ivan understood. Because Jared shared some of the burden of caregiving with others, he was able to continue to do it well for years to come.

Getting support when we need it allows us to continue to provide care to our loved ones over time, for as long as they need it, and to take care of ourselves.

CHAPTER 18

Listening, Sharing, and Paying Attention

A caring heart that listens is often more valued than an intelligent mind that talks.
—Michael Josephson

Many disagreements arise from our struggles as caregivers to attend to the needs of others. Often, our own needs and anxieties drown out our ability to truly hear what our loved one is communicating. When we listen mindfully, thoughtfully considering the other person's experience, we discover that responding in a heartfelt way isn't hard at all. Instead of a missed opportunity, we create a meaningful connection.

After a few years of helping her aging parents, who lived a half hour drive away, Val is relieved, perhaps even excited, at the prospect of them moving in with her and her family.

She is surprised at her feelings because not long ago, none of them—her parents, her family, herself—would have thought it a good idea. Her parents have always been independent-minded people, and Val has a busy life with her husband, her children, and a challenging work schedule. She knows that her father can be demanding and her mother tends to be high strung. But, lately, when Val would ask about medical appointments, her parents would respond in vague, dismissive tones. At the end of the month, her dad would tell her that he didn't have enough money to cover their bills, but he would give her a hard time if she suggested she take them over. Val was beginning to feel concerned about their welfare and unable to be of much help.

When Val and her husband decided to buy a larger house, they made sure it had enough room for Val's parents. Then they sat down and had a calm, measured conversation in which Val, her husband, and her parents could all express their needs and concerns about the move. Val's father was notably relieved that, in selling their home, he would have enough money to pay his remaining bills. Val's mother looked forward to family dinners a couple of nights a week, though not every night. They agreed that Val's parents could pitch in by occasionally babysitting, driving the grandkids, and preparing dinner. They all agreed that they would continue to talk about how things were going and what they each needed, rather than feel trapped or resentful.

With their new efforts at open communication and the creation of a clear plan for living in one house, all involved can feel reassured that they are all part of the same team. Val isn't under any illusions that it will all be perfect, but they are off to a good start. What was a worry has become a joy.

Communicating with patience and respect, allowing for give-and-take, and encouraging the expression of needs and desires can make the caregiving relationship more manageable and even joyful.

On several occasions, often while Jonathan was in a meeting at his law firm, he'd receive panicky calls from his father, claiming that he had fallen down.

Jonathan would rush to his father's apartment, only to find his father looking unharmed but happy to see him. If he had fallen, it had been pretty minor. Jonathan would feel relieved but resentful, and also concerned about whether his boss would continue to allow him to leave work to care for his father. On the third occasion, Jonathan, again finding no apparent harm, let his father know how irritated and stressed he felt. The crestfallen expression on his father's face made Jonathan rethink the situation. Maybe the panic hid something else. Maybe spending long days alone was not working for his father.

Jonathan began a practice of calling his father mid-morning every day to check in. They'd talk for about ten minutes and finish the conversation with a plan for when they'd next speak or meet. Jonathan also arranged for a housekeeper to visit his father's home after that mid-morning call to prepare lunch and do some light cleaning. Although his father protested at first, he came to enjoy the company and the meal. The panicky calls stopped, and Jonathan had the reassurance that his father was feeling calmer.

If we pay attention to the message behind the behaviors of our loved ones, we often learn that they have unmet needs. Then, rather than feeling irritated, we can focus on how to support them best.

JULIA:

I stepped through the door of my grandmother's apartment in the assisted living facility, thinking about the time she'd taught me to make stuffed cabbage.

The memory was clear, more than thirty years later: Her care, patience, and joy in teaching me the complex preparation had made me feel as if she held me in a special warm embrace. Now that she was in her nineties, with progressive dementia, she could no longer make the foods we all associated with her. She could do so little now.

I was smiling at the memory when I walked through that door, and she greeted me with a big smile in return. My grandmother no longer remembered my name, but she recognized me as a loving family member and patted the couch next to her. I sat down and held her hands. She looked at me with a happy face and asked me if it was my birthday. Although it wasn't, and although my grandmother no longer could show her care by doing things for her family, in that moment, she was able to make me feel that special warm embrace that only she could offer. She was always ready to celebrate those she loved.

Even when our loved ones' ability to contribute declines, if we are patient and attentive, we can relish what they still have to offer.

Wanda had been the preacher in a small neighborhood church for decades.

Wherever she went in town, people would stop her to ask for advice, to get the latest information, or to receive a blessing. She was always a strong woman who spoke her mind and made people feel loved, even as she chided them for bad behavior or cajoled them to participate in her services. People—even her own daughter, Tamika—loved and feared her.

When Wanda had a severe stroke and could no longer speak, the entire community was shaken. Tamika was determined to take care of her. The church elders met with Tamika to find out what they could do in their time of need. At first, Tamika had no idea. People had already dropped off enough food and sent cards and flowers. She was handling the caregiving just fine for now.

Then Tamika came up with an idea for something that would help Wanda. She contacted the elders and told them what she wanted to do. They organized it for the very next Sunday. When Tamika took Wanda to church that day to listen to another preacher's service, she helped her mother to the front of the church, where they sat down. Everyone lined up in front of Wanda. One by one, they told Wanda how she had helped them, and they thanked her for her loving care. Tears, laughter, and hugs filled the church. The service was the most powerful Wanda had ever attended.

Honoring our loved ones by sharing with them what they mean to us, how important they are to us, and how they have influenced us brings joy and love into the present moment.

Her high school friends sometimes asked Amelia if she resented having to go to her Grandma Marilyn's house after school each day.

They got to be carefree teenagers—playing sports, working on the school's online magazine, or just hanging out. Amelia, in contrast, was responsible for making sure that Grandma Marilyn was okay and then had to start making dinner until her mother, after leaving work, arrived at Grandma's house to complete the meal.

Fortunately, Amelia loved everything about her grandmother, especially her interesting stories about growing up in a big, boisterous family in a crowded city neighborhood. Rather than feeling resentment, she looked forward to sitting at the kitchen table, eating hazelnuts and ginger cookies, while Grandma Marilyn told her again about what it was like to live in their fifth-floor apartment with only one telephone and no television and few toys or books. There was the story of the Christmas when their tree caught on fire, and she and her five siblings had put it out by dousing it with eggnog. There was the story of Grandma Marilyn's own parents, European immigrants, who could sing folk songs in three languages.

Amelia felt that, through enraptured listening, she could learn about a different time and see what her grandmother had been like when she was her age. This was better than playing sports or hanging out; this was living history with someone she loved.

The bonds between grandparents and grandchildren are often sweet and strong. By attending to our older loved ones' stories, we learn family history, legacies, and values.

JULIA:

As my mother-in-law's dementia has worsened, she has had more trouble distinguishing reality from dreams and fantasies.

One evening, she was beaming as she told me that she'd recently walked to my house and had seen paper lanterns arranged in a large circle, lighting up my backyard. She had enjoyed the beautiful scene. I smiled back at her: She could barely walk through her apartment, not to mention a one-mile walk to my house. She was no doubt remembering the lanterns from New Year's Day, when our town traditionally lines the streets with paper bags filled with sand and candles. We had taken her for a drive to look at the lovely sight four months earlier.

Would it make sense to inform her of the impossibility of her experience? As I considered my response, looking at her smiling face, I couldn't find a good reason to insist that she differentiate this dream from reality. Certainly, it would be important on some occasions. But on this one, I just said, "That must have been a wonderful sight." She nodded, still smiling. We looked at each other warmly.

Any emotionally connected moment is worth savoring.
It can bring greater benefit than being right or being real.

CHAPTER 19

Love, Cherish, and Honor with Compassion

> *Just don't give up trying to do what you really want to do. Where there is love and inspiration, I don't think you can go wrong.*
> —Ella Fitzgerald

A loving attitude is a powerfully healing force. When hurt feelings and grief blind us, when loss devastates us, when we feel guilty for our impatience with those for whom we care, love can still guide our way through painful times. Making the compassionate effort to view circumstances from our loved ones' perspectives gives us the insight to work out differences and honor and care for them in the best way possible.

Mindy lay awake at 3 a.m., straining to hear if her husband, Ed, was breathing next to her.

She knew he was, but ever since the doctor had told them that he was in heart failure, she'd been waking up to listen. Her racing heart would make getting back to sleep challenging. Typically, she'd listen as hard as she could and would ultimately hear his breath going in and out. She'd feel reassured but would still have trouble falling back to sleep.

The diagnosis had been a surprise. Prior to that, Mindy had believed for several months that her husband was just being difficult and purposely walking more slowly. She had gotten irritated with him on numerous occasions, urging him to catch up with her. When she'd learned that his heart was actually the problem, she'd felt so guilty, even negligent; if she'd noticed his decline, they could have contacted the doctor sooner.

On this night, Mindy decided to listen for Ed's breathing as usual, but then she focused on her own. A slow breath in and a slow breath out, and then another and another. She acknowledged that she was feeling fearful about Ed, and guilty, but that she loved him intensely. She also acknowledged that she was human and made mistakes, but that she felt grateful to have Ed in her life. Then she concentrated on her own breathing—gently pushing all thoughts out of her mind—until she drifted off to sleep.

The stresses of life can lead us away from focusing on our feelings of gratitude, compassion, and love. Take the time to breathe, reflect, and remember to be mindful of these most valuable feelings.

JULIA:

After my father had a series of fender benders, my siblings and I decided that we couldn't allow him to continue driving.

His memory was declining, he'd suffered some strokes resulting in partially occluded vision, and at times, he'd become disoriented in the town where he'd lived for more than forty years. But none of us wanted to have that conversation with him. We all knew how painful it would be. Somehow, my siblings decided that I should be the one to bring it up.

My daughter had just gotten her learner's permit and had told my father how eager she was to get a car once she had her driver's license. When I finally gathered the courage to tell him—in a tone of great love and compassion—that we all agreed that he shouldn't be driving anymore, that we were worried about his safety and the safety of others, he stared at me in silence for a few moments. He finally said, "Let me think about it." I agreed, and gave him the time and space he needed to reflect.

The next day, while we were having lunch together at his house, my father offered his car to my daughter. He ceremoniously gave her the keys and told her about the engine and the type of oil it needed. She was overjoyed, and my siblings and I were relieved. His grace and generosity in that moment still brings tears to my eyes.

Showing compassion, love, and patience when discussing painful topics can bring out the best in everyone.

Gloria wanted to confront her mother about how she gave away her belongings to the aides who cared for her.

Each week, another item was missing. A small glass vase that usually held dried flowers had disappeared off a shelf. There were empty drawers where handbags had been stored. Shoes, still wrapped in the tissue paper in which they had been purchased, were gone. Gloria wasn't concerned about the items per se; she wasn't especially interested in most of her mother's things. She was uncomfortable about having no say in the matter. She'd hired the aides, who came in for two hours a day to fix meals and provide company for her mother. What was her mother doing without consulting her?

When Gloria finally got up the nerve to ask, her mother sighed and said, "But they're caring for me, so I try to care for them, too." The two of them looked at one another in silence for a few moments, as Gloria slowly began to see her mother's perspective. Always a proud, self-sufficient woman, her mother was still eager to maintain a little control over her life. She could decide how and when to appreciate the women who were providing her care. She could give them items that she no longer used or that she didn't mind parting with. This would allow her to feel better about receiving care.

Gloria gave her mother a hug and said, "What a nice thing to do."

Her mother smiled and added, "Don't worry. I have plenty of things for you, too."

Gloria took the moment to say, "Thank you."

Taking the time to consider the care recipient's perspective can help us to communicate in more caring and accepting ways.

After their husbands died, their respective children wanted them to move into their homes.

But Connie and Belinda, sisters only eighteen months apart, decided to honor a pact made long ago. When they were children sharing the same third-floor bedroom of their small family house, they had lain awake at night, telling secrets and swearing devotion to one another. After they'd grown up and had their own families in neighboring towns, they remained best friends. They hadn't always planned to spend their last years together, but it made perfect sense to them.

When Belinda's knee replacement surgery failed to decrease her severe arthritic pain, Connie moved into her house to help her with cooking, cleaning, and maintaining the home. Since Connie was also becoming more forgetful, Belinda helped her by organizing and paying her bills. Where one was weak, the other was strong, and they took care of one another.

Connie and Belinda, like most sisters, sometimes squabbled. But their adult children and grandchildren could see that the sisters deeply loved one another and felt gratified by caring for each other. They enjoyed dinner together every night, eating meals based on their mother's recipes, and had lively conversations. They shared memories of their parents, the old neighborhood, and school friends in ways no one else in the family could. They had the same private jokes, the same favorite songs. They were like an old married couple; one would start a sentence and the other would complete it.

As loving sisters, they were facing old age together with understanding, comfort, and joy.

Loving siblings with shared history and mutual devotion
can provide each other with a lifetime of support,
especially during the caregiving years.

BARRY:

During the years when my stepfather's dementia progressed, my mother found ways of loving him more.

He was unsteady on his feet and fell a lot. She would sit on the floor next to him, speaking calmly and tenderly until help arrived to pick him up. He was also unsteady in his mind and often confused and agitated. She would turn on the Turner Classic Movies channel, and the two of them would spend the afternoon sitting close together on the living room couch, lost in the musicals and dramas of their youth.

Later, when his falls led to a series of hospitalizations and his middle-of-the-night wandering frightened her, with a heavy heart, she placed him in a local nursing home. The nursing home was an old, antiseptic place, where my stepfather spent most of the next two years sitting in its crowded dayroom, staring blankly at his fellow residents across the dining room table.

My mother, to her credit, sat right next to him three days a week, oblivious to others, focusing all her attention on him. They didn't speak to one another much. He'd lost most of his powers of speech. When he tried to communicate with her in stammering garbled syllables, she bent her ear toward him patiently and strained to catch his meaning. Then she'd look into his blue eyes to try to read his mind. Most of the time, they sat in silence. She would pat his hand and wipe dried food from his worn sweatpants or straighten the collar of his tennis shirt. When his lunch tray came, she spoon-fed him his mashed potatoes and broiled chicken.

What struck me most about those days was the expression on my mother's face. She was content just to be with him, to look at him lovingly and protectively, to be absorbed in his presence. She always left the nursing home lighter and happier to have made contact with him. I've never witnessed such love toward any person in such a sad state. I've never witnessed such love toward anyone in any state.

We cherish our loved ones regardless of how illness and circumstances have changed them. The power of that love sustains them—and us.

Daisy's stepbrother, Ryan, made it clear that he and his wife should have first pick of his mother's furniture once she moved to the nursing home.

Although they had been step-siblings from a very early age, and Daisy had cared for her stepmother, Diane, as much as Ryan had, he didn't see her as his equal when it came to the furniture. Daisy wasn't exactly surprised; Ryan had often competed with her, although for the most part, they'd had a pretty good relationship.

Daisy had always loved a corner cabinet (she'd remembered hiding in it as a child), but she didn't want to fight with Ryan over Diane's things. But she felt resentful toward Ryan and found herself avoiding him. She was disappointed that his wife, with whom she'd been close for years, didn't speak up for her.

Diane's dementia and the frosty relationship with Ryan and his wife were making Daisy feel sad. She felt as if she were losing a lot all at once. Daisy decided to try to look at the situation a little more compassionately. She knew that Ryan loved Diane and was already grieving for her just as she herself was. When she thought about it that way, Daisy found that she could actually accept that Ryan wanted to hold on to what he could. She graciously let him know that she understood about the furniture. After some time had passed, Ryan asked her if she was especially fond of a piece or two. In the end, she was able to get the corner cabinet that reminded her of her childhood in Diane's house.

Practicing compassion helps us to understand and accept how others feel. Compassion can make interactions warmer and more successful in difficult, painful times.

Mindfulness

Keep your face always toward the sunshine—
and shadows will fall behind you.
—Walt Whitman

Focusing our energy on the present moment, the natural beauty around us, and the joy found in our relationships gives us a positive perspective on living. When we tune out the regrets from the past, the worries about the future, and inner tension, we feel peaceful and more optimistic. Breathe deeply. Reflect on the moment. Become aware. Feel at ease.

Wh en I awaken, I take a moment to clear my mind of worries and dread.

I take a deep breath. I feel the breath fill up my chest, and then I slowly breathe out. As I do so, I let go of the tension and anxiety and find the centered calm of slow, deep breathing.

This is my morning meditation.

I remember to feel grateful for what I have: A comfortable bed, a roof over my head, food for breakfast. I contemplate the many good aspects of my life and allow my feelings of appreciation to rise up as I continue to breathe.

I take a moment to appreciate the world around me: the sun peeking through my blinds, the blue sky, the birds chirping, the chill of autumn, and the falling leaves. Whatever the world outside holds, I remember to find my awe and breathe it in and out.

I reflect on how I would like to be on this day. I want to be positive, loving, compassionate, and strong. I want to feel good about myself and make others feel good, too. I breathe these feelings in and then release them to the world.

I will make this the best day possible. I will continue to breathe deeply and remember the profound feelings of this morning. I am now ready to start my day.

When you awaken in the morning, take a few moments
to center yourself with meditative breathing. You can
bring a profoundly positive focus to your day.

BARRY:

During the first night of her hospitalization, my mother was groggy and distracted—a lost child.

During the second, she was talkative and animated—a vibrant, commanding adult once again. During her third, she was greatly confused and agitated—a tormented soul.

"Who is this fluctuating person she has become in her struggles with dementia?" I asked myself. Who will she become? Will I know how to best help her? Where will tomorrow take us on this zigzagging journey?

As much as I pressed her doctors and nurses for answers, they were uncertain, too. Then one physician said, "Her disease and age have made her very fragile. You have to expect that she may change rapidly from day to day."

Expecting and accepting are not the same, though. I had to stop trying to force her to be the stable, strong-willed mother I knew. Since my birth, she had had to learn to adapt to how I changed as I developed from infant to toddler to youth to adult. I now had to learn to see her each time with fresh eyes and meet her wherever she was. She smiled today; I smiled back. She'll be quiet tomorrow; I'll sit by her quietly. The day after, she'll want to talk; I'll be there to chat.

When we have exhausted all our efforts to manage change, we simply strive to accept things as they are and will be. Doing so makes us focus on the present moment, not on our past notions or future hopes.

In that brief space of time between the early departures of her adult daughter and grandchildren for school and her husband's awakening, Sylvia hears them: the blue jay's caw, the cardinal's whistle, the purple finch's high trill.

In this large, busy house, where three generations care for one another, she savors the time when she sits by the window at the kitchen table with her second cup of coffee and has the luxury to listen and hear. She can still make out her husband's low snoring, too, from the back bedroom on the first floor, but she bends her ear to the calming, sweet bird songs.

In the last few years, Sylvia has had too few moments of such repose. Her husband, slowed by congestive heart failure, needs her help with grooming and dressing, to drive him to many doctors' appointments, and generally to keep him active. When her grandchildren get off the school bus in the late afternoon, they look forward to snacks and her help with their homework. Pulled in too many directions, she often feels she has never done enough for anyone. At the end of the day, she finds no sense of accomplishment and peace—only dread about tomorrow's schedule.

But tomorrow is also supposed to be sunny and mild. She will open the kitchen window wide and listen for the small birds she cannot see in the high branches of the surrounding beeches and oaks. They are reminders to her that—outside the turmoil and strife of family caregiving—the steady rhythm of nature goes on. She knows its music will uplift and animate her for the rest of the day.

In the midst of stressful days, seek quiet moments of repose and replenishment. Nature, in particular, can rejuvenate. Regularly turn your mind to the beauty around you.

Afar his wife's stroke, Dan found it very hard to get used to the silence between them.

Shirley had mostly recovered her ability to walk but not the ability to talk intelligibly; her words came out in a mixture of half syllables and other gibberish. The two of them spent time together holding hands while sitting on the couch watching television or listening to music. But they could no longer converse as they had for the first thirty years of their marriage.

Then Shirley's speech therapist showed Dan a sort of trick. Because the powers to process language and music are generally located in different areas of the brain, Shirley remarkably could still sing—haltingly but clearly belting out whole lyrics—even if she could no longer speak. Dan immediately put this to use. Every morning, after finishing breakfast, together he and Shirley would sing "On the Sunny Side of the Street," harmonizing on the chorus ("Life can be so sweet/On the sunny side of the street"). It was a silly, old song but they needed silliness and reminders of old times at this point in their lives.

The quality of the music they made, the intermingling of their voices, would fully absorb Dan's attention. They weren't Broadway stars, but the musical notes seemed to reverberate in their small kitchen, enveloping them. He felt more aware of the sweetness of her voice—of the sweetness of her character—than he had in years. After they would finish the song, there was a kind of hush and a sense of relief as they smiled lovingly at one another.

Music is a powerful medium for emotional communication.
It heightens our awareness of being together with loved ones
in the present moment. It creates joy in the midst of sorrow.

During the best of times in their family life, when their kids still lived at home and everyone was healthy, Cora had been a worrier.

She constantly compared her children to their schoolmates, dwelled on slights in her interactions with neighbors, and worried that she and her husband, Charlie, wouldn't have enough money to comfortably retire. Her mind was so filled with concerns about the past and future that she rarely focused on what was right in front of her.

It had taken until they were in their sixties—when Charlie was diagnosed with ALS—to finally bring her up short. Not that his progressive neurological condition wasn't cause for worry; if she allowed herself, she could obsess about what his steady decline would do to him and them. But because his disease had greatly slowed him down, the pace of her thinking seemed to slacken, too. Because his time was short, her mind seemed more concentrated on enjoying his presence every day.

To change her habit of worrying, Cora had taken intentional steps to train her mind. She took a course at the local YMCA in breathing and other meditative techniques to help her relax and increase her awareness. She gained skill in reining in her typically galloping thoughts to better be in the present.

Now as she sat on the porch with Charlie on warm, sunny days, she worked to remain focused on just being with him. She took in his shiny, green eyes, the measured cadence of his hoarse voice. As she pulled him up straight in his wheelchair, she was aware of the softness of his flannel shirt and the familiar smell of his aftershave. They talked a little and watched the traffic go by. It would be easy to worry about his coming death, but Cora was much more intent on engaging—and engaging him—in this moment. They were finally together—calmly, lovingly, fully.

The ability to be present, for most of us, takes practice. When we achieve it, we become more aware of our loved one's struggles and our own fears, but also the gratifying sense of closeness that can arise in every moment.

Taking a mindful walk can be both calming and rejuvenating.

The first step on your walk is to plan your path. You can walk around the block or walk in a park. Plan for as much time as you can spare. Wear comfortable shoes, sun protection, a warm hat and gloves in the winter. If possible, turn off your phone.

As you begin your walk, choose a slow, regular pace. Notice your breathing. Feel your breath go in and out as your chest raises and lowers. Look up at the sky and pay attention to its color. Is it a deep shade of blue, or light? Are there clouds? Where is the sun? Can you feel its warmth? Look ahead of you. Do you see trees? Notice the different colors. You can see so many shades of green if you look closely. Do you see flowers? If so, stop and look closely at one. The complexity of a flower is awe inspiring, if you take the time to study it. Are you walking by people, houses, or buildings? Wherever you are, pay close attention to the details around you. You will notice beautiful things that have been there all along.

If you become distracted during your walk, or begin to think about your responsibilities or stressors, remember that a wandering mind is natural. Just refocus on your breathing. Feel your chest raise and lower. Then begin again to look around at the many interesting sights as you walk slowly by. A mindful walk should give you respite from your daily stresses and remind you of the awesome beauty all around you.

Taking a mindful walk reconnects you with the world around you, providing perspective and peace.

CHAPTER 21

Optimism and Hope

Hope is being able to see that there is light despite all of the darkness.
—Desmond Tutu

Even when we encounter life's cruelest challenges, we have the choice to rise to the occasion. With an open heart and support from others, we can approach just about any situation with a positive attitude. When we do, we find that our optimism lights up the room and carries others along with us. No doubt, we will face painful times ahead, but by focusing on hope, we strengthen our ability to cope with whatever comes our way.

JULIA:

When my friend, Nina, was getting close to the end of a twenty-year battle with cancer, I visited her whenever I could.

Each time, I felt dread as the visit approached. I worried about how much worse she would look, how limited her movements would be, how we would find the words to discuss what was happening to her.

Each time I was joyfully surprised and relieved to find that Nina was her usual self, only with limitations. She could talk about anything, even her own upcoming death. She'd tell me her concerns about her children, who she worried about, even though they were mostly grown and doing well. She talked to me about her husband, worried about who would take care of him after she was gone and eager to be reassured that he would eventually move on. She discussed her medical frustrations and her physical limitations. Even as she struggled with pain, she loved to talk about foods she enjoyed, despite the choices becoming more and more limited. When she could no longer read, she listened to books on tape and watched television shows on her tablet.

Nina was such an inspiration to me during her twenty-year battle. She kept fighting and lived her life to the fullest. She remained optimistic until the end. Even then, she had hope for the rest of us. I'll miss her for the rest of my life.

The optimistic, positive attitude of our loved ones who fight against the odds and live life to the fullest remain inspirational even long after they are gone.

When Fran's husband, Fred, was diagnosed with pancreatic cancer, they had little time left.

He was immediately placed in hospice care. She took time off from work and spent each day with him, even climbing into the hospital bed with him when he could tolerate it. They talked about their marriage, their love for one another, what would happen to her after he passed, and everything else they could think of.

Prior to the diagnosis, Fran had almost reached her limit with Fred. He'd become reclusive, argumentative, and miserable. He'd reject anything fun or social that she suggested. Fran had even considered giving up and mentioned divorce to her friends. She loved Fred, but their marriage had become an unhappy series of negotiations. He spoke of retiring early and moving west, away from her entire family. She was contemplating not going with him.

When Fred learned how ill he was, Fran was completely distraught. She loved Fred dearly and did not want him to die. But the fact that Fred had cancer explained why he had become so difficult. He was suffering. She immediately forgave him for everything that had gone wrong between them and was determined to spend the remainder of his time by his side, repairing and enjoying their relationship. Their final few months together were filled with love and connection. Fran holds these memories as some of her most precious ones.

Even when we have worked our way into a bad spot in our relationship with our loved one, each day offers the opportunity to change course in a positive way.

Two sisters shared in the care of their mother, Grace, who had recently been diagnosed with mild dementia.

Loretta, the older of the two, generally accepted the fact of their mother's decline, although she was sad about it. Polly struggled with it. When her mother would forget a name or a date or say something out of context, Polly was easily frustrated and quick to correct her.

When the two sisters talked about their mother, Polly would express her hope that Grace would do better—that medication, healthy living, and good nutrition would improve her cognitive ability. Loretta would say that Grace would inevitably decline; although they might be able to slow it down, they should continue to enjoy her company for as long as possible. Polly felt that Loretta had given up hope. She'd say she longed for the old motherly relationship in which Grace gave her advice and corrected her mistakes. She was angry that Grace was changing.

As the sisters continued to discuss the situation, Loretta helped Polly see that they would have to be more parental as Grace declined. They could take their lead from her, as she'd been such a good, caring mother. Their mother's dementia wasn't only a loss; it was an opportunity to give back to her, to support each other, and to grow into their roles as caregivers. Despite their sadness, they could focus on the positive aspects of the situation. Over time, the sisters supported one another as they supported their mother.

When we focus on the positive, we can broaden our view of a challenging situation to include hope, which can help carry us through and strengthen our relationships.

Colin and Toby were determined to care for Colin's mother, Isobel, despite the numerous roadblocks and potholes in their path.

They had three young children. The oldest, Maria, eleven, had developmental delays, and the twin boys, eight, were a constant handful. Colin and Toby both worked hard at challenging jobs. Although Toby could work from home part of the time, Colin's job required travel twice a month for several days.

When Colin's mother had a stroke that left her slightly disabled, they didn't hesitate to move her in to what they called their three-ring circus. The twins went back to sharing a room, and Isobel got the bedroom on the first floor. Colin and Toby knew it wouldn't be easy. Isobel now had medical appointments to get to and visits from physical and occupational therapists. But they pushed on. When they faced a roadblock, when a medical appointment conflicted with both of their work schedules, they asked their neighbors for help. When they hit a pothole, when one of their kids got sick, Toby worked from home. When Maria needed to get to her behavioral therapy appointment, Colin used his comp time to take her.

Each day was a new challenge, filled with unexpected issues to overcome. Sometimes, everything went wrong and there was nothing to do but start over fresh the next day. Usually, though, they worked out the important things, and the family continued along their rocky road with a positive attitude and a feeling of optimistic teamwork.

A positive attitude, community support, and family teamwork can make even the most challenging circumstances manageable.

BARRY:

After my stepfather's many falls and my mother's pneumonia and mini-stroke, I would sit for long hours in the emergency room cubicles feeling miserable and drained.

All I could see around me was dismal—my subdued relative propped up in the hospital bed; steadily blinking monitors; shiny poles with bulging plastic bags of fluids and antibiotics. Glaring fluorescent lighting overhead numbed my brain. Feeling fearful and impatient, I watched the curtained doorway, waiting for the groups of white-clad, grim-faced physicians to finally arrive and repeat the same questions or utter the same cautions.

In those fraught moments, I sought hope for my loved one's condition, but even more, for ways of buttressing my own resolve. Then it occurred to me that I could choose to focus on the catastrophic circumstances and become more anxious. Or I could choose to see signs of the healing and calming powers of human beings.

It was the nurses who provided the balm. They'd come in to do their own clinical assessments, but they used humor and a light, conversational tone. They brought extra blankets, but it was their extra warmth of personality in this place of dire emergencies that cheered the room. I marveled at their friendly patter, their attentiveness and energy. By focusing on them and not the heart monitor's running graph and blinking numbers, I could hang in there—even feel inspired—for as many hours as it took.

We caregivers don't always have control over what happens to our loved ones, but we do have choices about what we attend to. Even in tough times, we can draw strength from others, if we have a mind to see those strengths

CHAPTER 22

Respect

To free us from the expectations of others, to give us
back to ourselves—there lies the great, singular power
of self-respect.
—Joan Didion

When, with compassion and humility, we truly respect other people, we can then better serve them and, in turn, ourselves. Understanding and accepting their needs, struggles, strengths, and weaknesses allow us to most fully appreciate their efforts, pain, and love. When we allow our loved ones to maintain their dignity, we perceive them most completely. This can only bring us closer to them and increase our own sense of self-respect.

JULIA:

On the supermarket checkout line behind my father, I took a slow, deep breath.

Riding up the conveyor belt was a six pack of beer and two boxes of cookies. There were meats and vegetables, too, but it was the beer and cookies that held my frustrated gaze. I let out that big breath and stopped myself from saying a word. We carried the shopping bags out to my car and drove back to his apartment. On the way, as he described the healthy meal we'd be making, I couldn't help thinking about his Type II diabetes and his progressive kidney disease. He already knew how I felt about certain items in his diet because we'd discussed it at least one too many times before. Was it my place to tell him how to live his life? Would he listen to me anyway?

Of course, I told him my thoughts. And he told me his. He felt that he was using moderation and good judgment and it was important for him to decide what he ate. I had to keep this in mind. I felt that I had to allow him to live his life his way as much as possible, while trying to keep him safe.

As caregivers, we need to balance our need to keep our loved ones safe with allowing them to maintain some control over their own life choices.

When Kanta had married Rob, she actually hit it off with his grandmother better than she did with any other family member.

She loved Rob's sisters and his parents, but she adored his Nunna. When Kanta would visit her on weekends to learn to cook her traditional dishes, she'd enjoy every minute with her. She'd carefully write out the recipes, and as they cooked, she'd listen to Nunna's stories about her life in Italy before she came to the United States. Although Kanta's own family was from India, the small-town stories would remind her of her extended family.

When Nunna was suddenly diagnosed with lung cancer, Kanta was as devastated as the rest of Rob's family. Kanta felt cheated, having had only a few years to spend with her. When Nunna made it clear that she did not want chemotherapy or any other intervention, Rob and his siblings and parents reacted strongly. They begged and pleaded with Nunna to follow the doctor's recommendations. But Nunna held fast.

When Kanta sat down alone with her to talk about it, Nunna explained that she had always feared doctors and hospitals. She didn't want to suffer terrible pain. Her beloved husband had died five years earlier, and she believed that it was time to join him. She felt she had lived a full and happy life and didn't want to struggle to extend it. Kanta couldn't help crying. But she understood, she told Nunna, and the older woman said Kanta's understanding meant a lot to her.

Kanta explained Nunna's feelings to the rest of the family. Although her relatives continued to try to convince the older woman to fight the cancer, they did their best to take her fears and wishes into account.

Even when it comes to difficult situations, when we take the time to listen to our loved ones, we can better treat them with the respect that they deserve.

Polly always felt she had to prove herself to her older brother, Bob, and her sister, Helen.

They were over a decade older than Polly and tended to treat her like the cute baby sister she had been while they were still living at home. The fact that their mother, Brenda, still coddled her only reinforced their impression of Polly as sweet but incapable.

Then Brenda fell down the cracked basement stairs of the old family home, breaking her leg and hip, and Polly moved in for an extended time to help her. Bob and Helen were delighted and thanked her. But when they later learned that Polly, while living there, was making unilateral decisions to spend their mother's money on major house repairs—a new staircase, roof, and kitchen—they were furious. They complained to their mother that Polly was spending her money profligately. They urged her to stop.

Polly felt hurt. She knew the decisions she was making were in their mother's interests and that her siblings' complaints were unfair. Instead of getting angry at them, though, she decided to reach out to them and be as transparent as possible. She wrote them a letter detailing the house renovations with justified costs. She invited them to visit and see for themselves the positive difference the renovations had made. She wanted to demonstrate to them that their mother was in good hands.

When Bob and Helen visited, they were cold at first. But they couldn't deny the house was in better shape, and their mother was more cheerful than she'd been in years. As Polly treated them with warmth, they began to relax. Their little sister, they were realizing, had grown up into a prudent, reliable, and caring daughter.

Caregiving for an aging parent presents opportunities for adult siblings to recast their relationships with one another and develop new mutual appreciation.

When Janelle, twenty-two, developed double vision and then was diagnosed with MS, her mother had an overpowering urge to protect her.

This was her child, Shirley said to herself, her only daughter. She needed to draw her close and care for her. To Shirley's shock and dismay, Janelle wouldn't cooperate. She wouldn't allow her mother to attend her medical appointments or get involved in the medical decision making. She refused to move back home, despite her mother's pleas. She was intent on remaining as independent as possible—a capable adult grappling with her health crisis.

At first, Shirley couldn't understand her daughter's motives and felt rejected. She pressured Janelle to share more of what the doctors were telling her. But her daughter was firm. She said sympathetically to her mother, "I know this is hard for you. But if I let you handle this problem for me, then I will have already lost the battle against this disease to preserve who I am."

Her words were jarring. Shirley suddenly saw Janelle in a different light. She was impressed that her daughter could be so clear and determined at a time when she—her wise mother—was panicked. She would respect Janelle's wishes. More importantly, she had new respect and pride for the resolute young woman her daughter had become.

Illness tests and sometimes alters our family relationships. Through our loved ones' display of bravery and determination during crisis, we may gain newfound regard for them.

When Kerry's cancer came back for the third time, this time in her spine, she knew that the end of her life was in sight.

Her son and daughter, their spouses, her grandkids, and her friends all pushed her to travel to places she'd always said she'd wanted to visit. When she shrugged off their suggestions, they persisted, assuming that she only required encouragement. They wanted her to enjoy what was left of her life to the fullest. They pooled money to help her pay for her travels. But Kerry realized that she no longer wanted to travel.

At first, Kerry was flattered that they wanted her to enjoy the time she had left by fulfilling her dreams. Then, after trying to make her feelings clear, she gradually became impatient when they continued to show her travel videos and highly rated tour companies. Finally, Kerry called a meeting of her family and close friends. She announced that she wanted them to listen carefully. She then explained that her wishes had changed. Although travel had always been something she'd longed for, at this point in her life, it was no longer her priority. With such limited time left, she wanted to spend as much time as possible close to home with the people she loved—them.

After a stunned silence, her family and friends agreed to support her wishes. Her daughter tearfully explained that they just wanted to do whatever they could for her. Kerry acknowledged and appreciated that. Then she reiterated that what she wanted was to spend her time with her loved ones. This time they heard her.

Our loved ones' needs and wishes can change as their life circumstances change. When we listen carefully and respect their wishes, we can meet their needs most successfully.

CHAPTER 23

Rewards of Caregiving

If you find it in your heart to care for someone else, you will have succeeded.
—Maya Angelou

When we care for another person with an open heart, our spirits lift and we have a deepened sense of meaning in our own lives. We become more competent and confident and may even feel redeemed for past behaviors. We feel valued, connected, and awed by a sense of personal transformation. Even after caring for a loved one comes to an end, we hold these experiences closely in our hearts.

After Bruce's mother passed away, he realized that he felt a little depressed.

It was more than just grief, which he'd experienced often. He had cared for her for seven years, during which he had given up many of his social activities and had fallen off the promotion track at work. He wasn't feeling resentful. On the contrary, he had made conscious decisions all along the way to put her care first. He felt extremely good about this. But after having devoted so much time and effort to caring for his mother, he felt adrift now that she was gone.

As a caregiver, Bruce had learned much. Not just how best to take care of his mother's needs, but the resources to help him do it. He had learned about hospitals, rehab facilities, doctors, medications, evaluations, community agencies with the best aides, and so much more. He'd developed a sense of confidence along with his competence. He recognized that the caregiving he'd done had changed him. He wasn't sure what to do next. He just knew that he needed to do something meaningful.

One day, while at his local public library, Bruce saw a flier about a talk someone was giving. It occurred to him that he could offer to give a talk about elder care. He asked the librarian if there might be a need for that, and she thought there would be. They set a date. Bruce was eager to share his experiences and knowledge and to give others an opportunity to do the same. He felt optimistic that this first talk might lead to others.

Caring for our loved ones can deepen a sense of meaning in our lives and bring a sense of competence and confidence that leads to positive growth and the desire to help others.

With a mixture of pride and apology, Rachel refers to herself as the family's black sheep.

Her three older siblings spent their teens and twenties going to school, finding mates, and preparing for successful futures, while she suffered from learning disabilities and clinical depression and floundered. She was embarrassed and burdened by how much her parents worried about her. She pulled away from the family, drifting for years from city to city, in and out of colleges and low-paying jobs, from one relationship to the next. She felt like a failure, often saying, "I'd felt ashamed that I couldn't please my parents."

Then her father, once vigorous, was diagnosed with metastatic prostate cancer. Rachel shocked her mother and siblings by announcing she was coming home to help take care of him. "My father's cancer became a test for me to prove my love to them and also my competence as an adult," she said.

At first, her father was wary, unsure whether Rachel would bolt when caregiving became difficult. But with quiet persistence, she took up her new duties as family driver, cook, and advocate with the oncology team. When her father's cancer spread and he was in greater pain, she redoubled her efforts to comfort him with actions and words. Her mother was grateful. Her siblings stopped talking down to her as their troubled little sister and began regarding her with respect.

"I knew that, one way or another, I wouldn't be in this role forever," said Rachel, "but I intended to do what I could while I could to help them. This helped me."

For many family members, caregiving is seen as a golden opportunity for redemption. Through giving back, living down old family reputations, and demonstrating newfound talents, we create our own personal transformations.

Sally was eager to take care of her mother, Ava, especially because she was confident that she could make a difference, having worked as an occupational therapist for years.

Now that Ava was finally home, after the hospitalization and then rehab to help her recover from her stroke, Sally was determined to continue the rehab. Ava had already recovered some use of her arm and her language was returning. All she needed was some hard work.

Sally was unhappily surprised by the struggles she encountered. She'd seen some of these behaviors at work but had never imagined she'd have to manage them with her mother. Ava got worn out quickly, especially at first, and then she'd want to give up. She often became bored with the efforts and tried to focus on Sally's needs. She asked to skip exercises, saying she'd rather do something fun. And most surprising, Ava became angry at Sally, telling her daughter to leave her alone.

To keep pushing her mother along, Sally tried to treat her more like one of her patients. She wouldn't take no for an answer; she'd offer rewards for finishing tasks; and she'd put on her upbeat, cheerleader act. These efforts made Ava withdraw entirely and absolutely refuse to do anything. Sally found herself in tears.

She decided to take an entirely new tack. She asked Ava what she wanted to work on and when. She let Ava run the show. Sally realized that doing rehab with a loved one was complicated and required sensitivity. Ava responded immediately and worked hard, and the progress she made, though slow and arduous, was rewarding for them both.

Caring for our loved ones can be challenging. If we persist, reflect on our efforts, and try new approaches when the old ones fail, our care can be valuable both to our loved ones and to ourselves.

When Samantha stopped by with a casserole or a treat, Mrs. Richards usually took a while to get to the door but when she pulled it open, there was always a big smile on her face.

Samantha's own mother had passed away when she was twenty-four. Now at fifty-three, an empty nester, she enjoyed playing daughter to Mrs. Richards, whose only child, a son, lived across the country.

They had become friends, confidants, and practically family. Samantha made a habit of shopping for Mrs. Richards when she went food shopping for herself, often choosing special treats like the ripe peaches she'd found at the farmer's market. They'd go on outings to see gardens, stroll slowly in a park, or go to a matinee movie. If Mrs. Richards needed help with something, she knew she could ask Samantha. Samantha could tell Mrs. Richards her worries about her grown children, her thoughts about the future, even complain about her husband a little. She enjoyed hearing Mrs. Richards' stories from her life, too. They often laughed together about the silly things people did.

When Samantha and her husband had moved in next door to Mrs. Richards several years before, she was hoping to make friends in their new neighborhood. That had happened. But she had never imagined she'd find such joy in her friendship with a woman so much her senior. What a wonderful surprise.

When we open our hearts to care for others, and allow them to care for us, we can find joy and meaning in the connections we make.

In the recent past, since her mother's dementia had worsened, Meredith had felt a bit sad and lonely on her birthday.

Her mother used to make such a big deal about it each year but couldn't do much anymore. No family was nearby to celebrate with her, although she got some e-mails, cards, and texts. She spent so much time caregiving that she had few close friends.

Yet a few years before, Meredith had decided to take action rather than just feel down. Now, each year, she went about the day as usual, except that she stayed mindful of any opportunity to do small favors for people. Last year, when she stopped at the bank, she held the door open for an older couple and let them get in line in front of her. They were grateful. As she walked out to her car at the grocery store, she stopped to help a woman put her groceries in her trunk. The woman thanked her profusely. When she arrived home to her mother, she put flowers she'd purchased in a vase on the table. Her mother smiled. Meredith reminded her mother that it was her birthday, and together they celebrated over a nice dinner and a store-bought cake.

Her mother no longer remembered Meredith's birthday, but that didn't stop Meredith from feeling good about herself and from helping others, which, in turn, made her feel even better.

When we feel down, we can offer caring and kindness to others.
The smiles, gratitude, and connection we receive in return
lift the spirit and are rewarding.

CHAPTER 24

Sacrifice

*Two things awe me most: the starry sky above me and the
moral law within me.*
—Immanuel Kant

Responsibility, guilt, feelings of indebtedness, an opportunity to give back—these are some of the personal reasons we
commit ourselves to the work of caregiving. When we derive
meaning from the sometimes difficult sacrifices we are required
to make, providing care becomes easier. When we truly recognize that we are sustaining our loved ones through the support
and comfort we bring, we feel enriched by the experience. These
rewards are fulfilling and lasting.

You've meant so much to me," Claire, forty-seven, says to comfort her crying mother.

The older woman cries not only because she recently suffered a paralyzing stroke, but because she feels humiliated about burdening her only daughter. Claire hopes her words will convey several sentiments: You have given me so much throughout my life. I'm grateful and want to give back to you now. Who you are and will be still means a great deal to who I am.

When caring for loved ones is simply going about the business of completing necessary tasks to meet present needs, it can lack the depth of meaning and feel like an unsustainable burden. Caregiving is best grounded in the history of the relationship, complex as it may be. If, on the whole, we can remember and cherish our loved ones' part in our lives, their good character and virtuous deeds, then despite the responsibilities, our caregiving can have a reason and emotional resonance that infuse us with purpose and love. What we do for our loved ones, we do to honor their past efforts and our own best selves.

Through finding and holding on to those sustaining memories, we bolster our efforts to give care. If the rigors of caring have consumed us and we have forgotten those better, bygone days, then we need to dig deep to see who we are and to see our choice to give care today in the context of a lifetime of receiving from others.

Strive to view your caregiving as an opportunity for giving back.
You will see your work as the fulfillment of a loving relationship—
enriching, not depleting.

There are days when taking care of his bedbound wife, who had suffered a stroke, exhausts Bob's body and saps his will.

He awakens each morning with apprehension, thinking of all he'll have to do: groom and feed her, clean up the apartment to her high standards, and watch the evening TV shows she likes. He collapses into his own bed each night feeling regret for all he has had to give up to serve as her caregiver—a successful job as a realtor, his close group of male friends, the carefree times he used to spend hanging around the house or reading magazines at Starbucks. He has chosen this role—chosen to make these sacrifices—but keenly feels the loss of his old, comfortable life.

What sustains him and makes the sacrifices bearable? "Throughout our marriage, she's taken good care of me," he says. "When I had an alcohol problem, she literally pulled me out of the bars. She helped me get sober. I want to give back to her." That memory and the debt he feels he owes her fuels his caregiving every day.

But there's another reason. "If something were to happen to her, I'd feel very guilty," he says. "I don't want that kind of guilt." In his face, there's a hint of anguish at the very thought that she might suffer greater physical pain, causing him to suffer emotional pain.

The clincher for him is yet simpler. "No one else will step up to take care of her," he says. "Not her kids from her first marriage. Not her sister. I'm the only one who cares enough." That fact is plain to him. It means he bears responsibility. He takes that responsibility seriously. He can endure the sacrifices because his sense of purpose is indomitable.

Caregiving entails many difficult sacrifices. We shouldn't dismiss the impact of those sacrifices. But we must find personal reasons to justify—and bolster—the choice to give up part of our lives for the benefit of our loved one.

Christina's husband, Ben, was having a hard time accepting the amount of time that she was devoting to caring for her father.

He wanted her dad to be safe and comfortable, too, but he felt that Christina was going too far. He felt that she was neglecting her marital relationship. When he'd bring it up, she'd get annoyed and tell him he just didn't understand. They'd both quietly fume in separate rooms for the rest of the evening.

Christina was determined to avoid placing her father in a nursing home. Long ago, she'd promised him that she'd never do that. He had been there for her when she'd gone through tough times. Although he needed a lot of help physically, his mind was still clear. He lived just a few minutes away, so she stopped by his home before work, during her lunch hour, after work, and once again to help him to bed. She didn't mind because he was so grateful and cooperative and always glad to see her. What was difficult for her was being home with her husband, who seemed angry with her much of the time.

One evening, Christina asked Ben to sit down with her. She tried to explain to him why caring for her father was so important to her. She also made it clear that she understood how it had affected their lives. Then she invited Ben to help her. Would he go with her now and then? Or even take her place on occasion? Ben considered what to do. Although it wasn't easy, he chose to accept that, for now, a large part of their lives would focus on caring for Christina's father. By joining her in her efforts, Ben could be more supportive of his wife and share in her mission. Christina was grateful that he chose to try to understand and help her. She vowed to support him when he needed that from her.

Sacrifice is always involved when we do the hard work of caregiving. Supporting one another in our efforts brings us closer together.

Maryann couldn't believe her bad luck—a ticket to a great concert and an invitation to a beach party on the same weekend that she had agreed to care for her mother.

There was no way out; it was definitely her turn. Her older sister—who had young children to care for—had spent the previous two weekends with their mother. Maryann had no one to care for but herself. She hated to miss fun events to sit with her mother, but she had metastatic melanoma and couldn't be left alone. She anticipated a depressing weekend ahead.

Feeling miserable, she turned down the invitations and headed to her mother's apartment. She'd brought an MP3 full of music and some fashion magazines to read, figuring her mother would be sleeping a lot. At least Maryann would keep herself entertained.

To her surprise, her mother was overjoyed to see her. Despite her limited energy and need to take periodic naps, her mother was eager to sit with Maryann, listen to her music, and look at her magazines. They spent the weekend talking, laughing, and feeling connected. Maryann painted her mother's toenails while they listened to music from one of the groups that was playing at the concert she was missing.

Long after her mother's passing, Maryann remembered that weekend with such gratitude and love that it would bring tears to her eyes. She wouldn't have missed it for the world.

When we sacrifice our own wishes and longings, and give to those we love, what we receive in return is lasting and priceless.

Donald was the only one of his siblings to repeatedly run away from home, to drop out of high school, to cause the police to come to the door late at night, and to continue living in the same town as his parents long after his siblings had all moved away.

Years after he had become an upstanding citizen, Donald felt guilty for what he had put his parents through. They, on the other hand, had long ago forgiven him for his teenage behavior and were relieved he was doing well.

When his mother developed dementia and his father needed help with her care, Donald was right there, ready to do whatever they needed. He took over chores his mother had done, stayed at the house with her while his father went to meet with friends or see a ballgame, and drove them both to appointments. He made meals for them, boxing up the leftovers for reheating the next day. He managed to keep his job as a mechanic, at least for the time being, since he could cut back his hours and work flexibly because his boss knew Donald's parents needed him. As his mother's symptoms got worse and his father needed more support, Donald worried that he'd have to quit the job.

Donald felt sad about his mother's decline, but he felt joy, practically to the point of tears, about having the opportunity to give back to his parents and to stand by them as they had stood by him. He was willing to devote his time to them because he knew it was for the most meaningful and important effort of his life.

When we understand our caregiving efforts as meaningful, we are willing to make sacrifices to do what our loved ones need because we know that we are bringing joy and comfort to them as well as to ourselves.

CHAPTER 25

Seek Out Other Caregivers

Communication leads to community—that is, to
understanding, intimacy, and mutual valuing.
—Rollo May

Usually, we can do the hard work of caregiving on our own. But should we? Through reaching out to others who struggle with the same issues and understanding our dedication and frustrations, we gain a feeling of connection, validation, and support. We discover that others share our values and commitment. We learn from their experiences and share our own. We feel relief that we are not so alone after all.

At first, Charles went to the caregiver support group only to placate his wife.

On several occasions, she'd left notes for him with the dates, times, and locations of the group's next meeting. He knew why she wanted him to go. Caring for his father since his Parkinson's disease had gotten so much worse was challenging. His father had never been an especially kind or patient man, even without his current physical limitations. His fuse had become very short, especially with Charles.

Finally, Charles relented. He walked into the room at the hospital that evening to find a small gathering of people eating cookies and holding coffee cups. He helped himself. As they all began to sit down, several people said hello and welcomed him. The facilitator, a young woman, began the meeting by getting updates from some regulars. Each one had major challenges to deal with. After several others told their stories, the facilitator asked Charles if he'd like to speak. He took a breath and found himself talking to a room full of strangers about his relationship with his father.

The group listened until he was done and then offered supportive words. A few people shared similar experiences. No one gave him advice; no one told him what he should do. But they seemed to know what he was talking about. Charles felt grateful to them. Afterward, on his way out, one of the other men put a hand on Charles's shoulder and said, "I hope we'll see you next time." Charles thought, "They just might."

Sharing our stories with other caregivers who understand our feelings and who have had similar experiences can be a great support as well as a relief.

Bob's wife, Dora, had always been a bit flaky. Over their many years together, he'd often teased her about it.

Lately, she'd become more confused and forgetful. She would leave the lights on or the front door open. Once, he found a burner on the stove going full blast, hours after she'd made dinner. That startled him. He decided that he needed to keep a better eye on what she was doing and check up on her a bit more. But the situation kept getting worse.

Just before their daughters were supposed to arrive for a visit, Bob found Dora wearing a colorful blouse two sizes too big and no pants at all. She had put on so much makeup that she looked more like a clown than the lovely woman he had married. He hurried to help her clean up and find appropriate clothing. The last thing he wanted was to worry their daughters. They had busy lives of their own.

What he didn't know was that the purpose of his daughters' visit was to discuss getting some help for him in caring for their mother. They could see that she was growing more forgetful and becoming too much for him to handle alone. They asked if he would allow them to have someone come in who could be a companion for their mother; he could have a little time to himself and she could have a friend. It would mean a lot to them to help by screening applicants and finding someone they all liked. He resisted at first, insisting that he could manage by himself. Finally, he reluctantly agreed to try it.

As time passed and caregiving became more challenging, Bob became grateful for the few hours of relief the companion provided. He could talk to her about his wife's care. The brief periods off allowed him to continue to care for his wife for quite a long time.

Allowing others to help us care for our loved ones gives us time for rejuvenation. Having other caring people to talk to who know our loved ones and who support our efforts is also valuable.

Donna resented it whenever her daughter's pediatrician suggested she attend a support group.

Yes, she'd admit, it was sometimes hard to care for a young child with autism. That didn't mean she needed support. Donna felt she was coping just fine. She was enjoying her daughter, not feeling afflicted by her.

In truth, shy Donna had never felt comfortable joining groups of any kind—not as a Girl Scout, prom planning committee member, or block association captain. But when she was asked to help organize a fund-raiser to buy speech therapy workbooks for her daughter's school, she decided the project's worthiness should probably outweigh her reluctance. She tentatively agreed. At the planning group's first meeting, she sat to the side and mostly listened. Much of the talk focused on community outreach strategies for donations. During the conversations at the breaks, she found that the other mothers in the room had similar experiences and feelings as her—love for their children, frustration with their behavior at times, and aggravation with how little others understood autism.

By the next meeting, Donna was more engaged and talkative. She was freer with observations and frustrations from her own life. The other women in the room responded positively. Going to a support group hadn't appealed to her, but advocating for an important cause with her peers felt right. She was proud when the fund-raiser was a success. When other opportunities arose to get together with these mothers to fight for their children's education, she said yes with relish.

Talking about personal issues in support groups isn't for everyone. Sometimes advocacy—standing shoulder to shoulder, rallying for the same cause—brings us closer together.

Elliot, thirty, loved his longtime partner, Sharisse, twenty-six, but didn't love all he had to do to take care of her.

Since the diving accident four years earlier that severed her spinal cord and paralyzed her from the waist down, he helped toilet, groom, and dress her every day before climbing into his delivery truck for long hours behind the wheel. He was tired of the daily grind. And he felt alone. No one he knew their age was dealing with the same kinds of challenges. He drove in silence most of the day, brooding and worrying.

Sharisse worried about him, too, and suggested he join the caregiver support group at the rehabilitation hospital where she had physical therapy. But Elliot declined, saying that he felt shy talking about himself in front of other people. Instead, he started exploring resources online, where he could get support but remain anonymous.

On the Caregiver Action Network website, he started reading the forums, where caregivers around the country posted questions and answers about fatigue, depression, and frustration. On the Family Caregiver Alliance and Well Spouse Association websites, he learned about the telephone support groups these organizations run and then joined and began listening regularly. Much of what other caregivers said struck chords with him. He wasn't so alone after all.

Elliot still wasn't ready to talk about himself, but one day he decided to post a response to a question another caregiver had asked about how to buy a wheelchair. There was nothing personally revealing about the information, but he felt good when the person who asked the question thanked him. He was taking the first steps to join a larger community where he could offer help and, one day, ask for help.

Family caregivers have myriad ways to reach out to others for support.
Once connected, family caregivers share the kinds of practical suggestions
and heartfelt reflections to shore up one another.

Miriam wondered why Pastor Steve had asked her to join the church's new senior ministry group.

She always liked serving others and ordinarily enjoyed making meals for sick, older congregants. She was just surprised that her pastor seemed to think she should help others even more now, when he had noted concern that her husband's recent hospitalizations for congestive heart failure had worn her out.

She began to understand his thinking when she attended the group's first organizational meeting. Sitting in a circle in the church basement were a dozen other middle-aged women who seemed similar to Miriam. Some she knew from worship services and other church ministry groups as kind, friendly people. Others she met for the first time and learned that they were also taking care of aging parents or husbands who were disabled. All seemed to place a high personal and spiritual value on caring.

In the next few months, as the group met weekly to cook meals together and then deliver them to seniors in their homes, Miriam's relationships with the other women deepened. As they worked side by side, she heard their stories of caring for relatives and shared her own. Most of the older congregants they visited were widows, living alone. Driving back to the church, she heard many of the group members express gratitude that they themselves were not yet alone and that they still had their husbands or parents to care for.

Miriam felt the same. She was thankful every day to wake up next to her husband. As Pastor Steve had probably intended, she also felt grateful for these new friends and comrades in arms who supported one another in their good works.

When we find others who share our values and commitment to caring, we feel heartened.

CHAPTER 26

Stress Management

A good laugh and a long sleep are the two best cures in the doctor's book.
—Irish proverb

The often long process of providing care for a loved one can take a toll on us as caregivers. The unexpected crises, frequent frustrations, feelings of loss of control, and the losses, in general, wear us down. When we make a practice of managing our stress through mindful meditation, regular exercise, good sleep hygiene, and engaging in creative acts, we rejuvenate ourselves. After we've had time for quiet reflection or creative expression, we return to our caregiving tasks reenergized and more prepared to take on whatever new challenges arise.

Mindful relaxation requires practice.

If you make it a habit, you'll get better at it and you will reap the benefits. You should feel more relaxed, more grounded, more aware of your surroundings, and more able to handle the stressors that come your way. Find fifteen minutes each day to sit in a comfortable chair, close your eyes, clear your mind, and focus on your breathing. When thoughts about responsibilities, chores, interactions, or anything else enter your mind, gently push them away and refocus on your breathing. Try to maintain your focus. When you notice thoughts reappearing, let them go and refocus. Imagine your thoughts drifting away as you breathe in and out. Just breathe.

Practicing mindful relaxation for just fifteen minutes a day should make a difference in your life. You'll notice a sense of peacefulness as your body learns to slow your heart rate, lower your blood pressure, and quiet your mind. When you get better at this practice, you'll become able to call it up when stressors appear so that you can handle them with a sense of calm. The first step to a more mindful life is claiming that bit of time each day for yourself.

Take the time each day to practice mindful relaxation
in order to ground yourself and prepare for the day ahead.

In the past, when Florence took daily walks at her rheumatologist's urging to manage her fibromyalgia pain, her husband, Vince, often accompanied her.

It was an important way for them to stay fit and also have long, relaxed conversations about their life plans. But after arthritis caused swelling in her knees and she could no longer walk long distances, Vince gave up walking, too, so she wouldn't feel bad that he was still physically capable while she was not. Their days became housebound, dominated by TV and solitaire on the computer.

Then Vince's doctor urged him to begin a physical exercise regimen, the better to stay strong to care for Florence. The doctor explained that regular cardio workouts would maintain Vince's muscle tone and bone strength as he aged, while also keeping his mind sharp.

Vince was impressed but still hesitant. The notion that he'd stroll the neighborhood while leaving Florence home alone made him feel guilty. But he brought up his doctor's suggestion with her anyway. She was more supportive than he'd anticipated. "No one is a bigger believer in the health benefits of walking than I am," she said. Florence also came up with the idea of having friends and neighbors stop by to visit her when he was out.

Vince started walking two days a week, gradually increasing the distance that he covered. He took photos with his phone of flowering trees and interesting-looking houses along his path to show to Florence when he arrived home. He found that the exercise made him feel stronger and more relaxed. It always put him in a good mood, ready to engage Florence and care for her needs once again. The walks were good for both of them.

Physical exercise has benefits for caregivers' bodies and minds.
The dividends it pays in increased energy and resilience are
worth the investment in time and effort.

BARRY:

When frustrated, some guys chop wood or hit a bucket of golf balls.

I write. I don't exactly pound away at my laptop keys with the force of wielding a golf club, but I want my words to have power—to express my experiences. I turn on my computer, open my caregiving diary file, and let my emotions pour through my fingers and onto the screen in a rapid stream of consciousness. I write about feeling aggravated after waiting with my mother in a doctor's office for hours, feeling moved by a home health aide's kind act, feeling sad about my stepfather's vacant stare. When I close the file ten, fifteen, or sometimes thirty minutes later, I feel calmer and more grounded.

Writing's benefit for managing stress isn't only because it provides emotional catharsis. I could just as easily vent to my wife or bellow in my backyard at the top of my lungs. Writing captures my feelings in a form that I can easily review later and gain perspective about myself and the changes in my family's life. Often, I will wait weeks or months before rereading an entry. Then I'll wonder why I reacted so strongly to a given situation, when I might have been more patient. Or I'll realize how circumstances have gradually changed beyond my notice. I gain insight into my strengths and weaknesses as a caregiver and person. Through this kind of reflection, I learn, grow, and hopefully become a better person.

Caregiving journaling experts such as B. Lynn Goodwin and Margery Pabst recommend that caregivers get in the habit of writing regularly, even just short passages. They also suggest writing without a self-critical eye: Just do it. No experience or sentiment is too inconsequential to chronicle.

When your loved one dies and your work as a caregiver is done, these writings will be a cherished personal record of the challenging but often enriching caregiving years.

Writing is an important tool for coping with many of life's adversities. Take the opportunity regularly to put your caregiving experiences into words and gain perspective.

Sleep is restorative. It allows your body to recover from the stresses of the day.

It allows your immune system to work more efficiently. Sleep clears out toxins from the brain and improves memory. It is a crucial part of self-care.

Unfortunately, caregivers often struggle with sleep. Late at night, our minds can race with worries and fears we don't have time for during the busy day. We can feel wide awake, just as we should be settling down for a good night's rest. The next day, we can feel exhausted and irritable, and struggle to provide the best care we can. Over time, we may begin to fear bedtime, anticipating the ruminating thoughts and anxious feelings. This pattern needs attention.

If you're having trouble getting a good and full night's sleep, here are our suggestions:

1. Schedule an appointment to get a physical exam and describe your sleep issues to your primary doctor.

2. Do not drink alcohol at night.

3. Don't eat for several hours before going to sleep.

4. Stop any caffeine use by 3 p.m.

5. Make your room dark and keep temperatures on the cool side.

6. For at least a half hour before getting into bed, refrain from using electronic devices.

7. Get some exercise during the day.

8. Go to sleep at the same time each night.

9. Wake up at the same time each morning.

10. Don't watch the news right before going to bed.

11. Don't talk on the phone late at night, unless it has a calming effect.

12. Don't leave the TV on all night long.

13. Give yourself time to wind down before getting into bed.

14. Do some stretching prior to getting into bed.

15. Listen to relaxing music before going to bed.

16. Listen to a guided imagery recording.

17. Put a drop of lavender oil on your pillowcase.

18. Practice clearing your mind by focusing on your breathing.

When we make time to do some self-care, we can improve our sleep hygiene and get the rest we need.

BARRY:

When I am pressured to do too much with too little help, I try to sit quietly for few minutes with my eyes closed and see in my mind a blue lake.

In my imagination, I stand at its edge watching patterned lines rising across its surface from a sudden shift in wind. Bright sunlight shimmers in reflection. The wavelets are changing, flowing energy. Fish jump and slap the water. Ducks paddle and dive. Swallows glide low. Dragonflies hover near the willows.

The imagery takes me back to a lakefront, when my father, long before his cancer, showed me how to skip flat rocks—five, six times!—atop the water. I can hear the zing of nylon fishing line I am casting out from my old spin casting reel. I am bending forward, my sneakers slipping on the wet rocks, as I try to catch minnows in the shallows with only my cupped hands. I am pushing off the shoreline in a tidy Sunfish sailboat on a blustery day.

I emerge from these short mental trips to the lake refreshed, as if I'd actually felt the cool, moist breezes on my face. For the rest of that day, I'm able to navigate my earthbound life with a lighter step.

Through visualization, we can focus our attention away from current troubles toward revitalizing scenes. Remember a favorite scene from your life and take a short mental trip there.

Maria gives unstintingly and without regrets to her family—a demanding husband whose MS is progressing, their three young children, and an aging mother.

But she has unbreakable rules for herself. With her family's blessing, she goes upstairs every Saturday at 1 p.m. to the spare bedroom she has turned into her watercolor studio and locks the door behind her. For the next hour, she draws on her memories of seashores, wooded landscapes, mountain trails, and formal gardens to put paint to canvas with feathery strokes.

"Sometimes I can hear my husband calling for me downstairs," she says. "Sometimes my children knock on the door because they need something. But I won't allow myself to be disturbed for that hour."

The hour provides her repose. In dabbing with a thin, soft brush at the blue, yellow, and brown hues, she finds a point of concentration away from the wants and worries of her family. In the pastoral scenes she lightly paints, she connects with a sense of the world's beauty, which normally eludes her when she is helping her husband get in and out of the bathtub, clearing a stack of plates from the dinner table, or puzzling over insurance forms. In this hour, in this space, she has created a respite from caregiving that is like a suspension of struggling. Her mind clears and she stands more upright. Then she puts the paints away and unlocks the door.

"I go back downstairs, replenished, to my caregiving duties," Maria says. "I can hold on for another week until my watercolor hour again."

We sometimes need to remind ourselves that we are more than loving family members; we are individuals in our own right who need to be nurtured. We must zealously and regularly protect time to enjoy and reflect.

CHAPTER 27

Trust Your Instincts

Trust thyself: every heart vibrates to that iron string.
—Ralph Waldo Emerson

We can't always know what is best for our loved ones. We try to keep them safe and healthy, while accommodating their desire to remain as independent as possible. Well-intentioned professionals, friends, and family offer advice. But, ultimately, we must rely on our own instincts to guide our care decisions. Sometimes we feel the need to bring in more support than our loved ones believe they need. Sometimes we have to allow them to make their own choices, even when we disagree. We try to make the best judgments we can at the time, while accepting our own limitations.

BARRY:

I wanted my mother to live as independently as she could in the years after my stepfather died, when she was mostly alone and contending with chronic pain and cognitive decline.

But there were times I was concerned about her safety, and we disagreed about what she could or couldn't handle.

A big issue was her pills. She wanted to set up her own pillbox, but after I showed her frequently that she made mistakes that could have led her to take too much medication, she deferred to my judgment. Another issue was her walker. She never believed she really needed it and felt silly pushing it around. Often, she left it in one room and walked into another. After she fell and hurt herself several times, she ultimately agreed to rely on it.

The biggest issue, though, had to do with her home health aides. She could see no reason to have these companions helping her out of bed, making her meals, or driving her to appointments. She felt infantilized and intruded upon. Each time I suggested we increase the aides' hours per week because she needed more help, my mother fought back hard. Eventually, though, she came to like most of the aides and allowed herself to be persuaded to spend more time with them.

With each struggle, my mother's protests always set me to wondering if I was being a wise or overly cautious son. I had to trust my judgment that what I was suggesting—sometimes insisting upon—was for her health and safety and would keep her living in her own apartment longer. With all the help she received, my mother managed well.

It is hard to overrule the judgment of a loved one for whom you are caring. Ultimately, though, you must trust yourself to exercise prudence and ensure safety and well-being.

Andrea and her brother, Larry, understand their aging father's need to hold on to his tough-guy image.

He is a large, proud man and a good father, who stood up to bullies and slackers while running his own successful contracting business for many years. He built their family home with his own two hands and wouldn't even discuss leaving it when their mother died seven years ago. But now, this fiercely independent man is falling—literally. Rheumatoid arthritis makes his gait unsteady. His shuffling feet trip on the frayed carpeting and chair legs. When he goes down, he gets hurt.

How can they help their father remain safe? Talking with him gets them nowhere; he just waves them off as if they are still kids. They don't have the power or stomach to try to force him out of the house. They have to admit that he is taking a principled stand—to live in the manner he, not others, chooses for himself, as long as he can.

"He's a hardheaded guy," Andrea says. "I think he can take a few dings." Larry frowns but agrees. They can do little but accept his choices and help him live on his own terms. Because their mother had always wanted to redecorate the house before she died, they are able to finally convince their father to let them put in new carpeting and move the furniture around so he is less likely to trip.

Acceptance is hard. Their dad continues to fall occasionally. He won't complain about his pain. They have to tolerate their discomfort in abiding his wishes and seeing him hurt.

To avoid guilt, caregivers often try every avenue to ensure a loved one's safety. But there are limits to what any of us can do without violating the dignity of the people we care for. Accepting our limits means we accept that events will take their course.

One night after dinner, while the rest of the family had begun to pack up leftover food and clean the dishes, Evan's grandfather, Larry, who had received a diagnosis for dementia, summoned Evan to the living room.

Larry took a seat in his favorite brown leather chair and motioned for Evan to sit on the adjacent love seat. He announced that he wanted to tell his grandson a story. Evan loved hearing his grandfather's stories about experiences in the army during the Korean War or their family ancestry.

On this occasion, Larry told Evan a story from the Korean War. He explained how he met one of his greatest friends when the two young soldiers were required to stay up all night keeping watch during a torrential downpour. Evan, as always, enjoyed the story and the insights it offered into his grandfather's early years. He thanked his grandfather, but Larry frowned. With his head down in embarrassment, Larry confessed to Evan that he wasn't going to be able to remember these stories for too much longer because his dementia was progressing.

At first, Evan didn't know how to respond. How could he console a man he loved when the inevitable result would be so devastating, exactly as Larry was anticipating? But Evan trusted his instincts. He told his grandfather how much he appreciated all the stories he had heard over the years and how glad he was to learn some of the amazing moments of Larry's life. Slowly, Larry looked up, smiled at his grandson, and began to tell another story.

Sometimes it can be difficult to know what to say to an ailing relative. But when we trust our instincts and speak from the heart, we can show our loved one how much we care.

When Sally's son, Anton, was born with severe physical deficits from cerebral palsy, she was bombarded with unsolicited advice from doctors, nurses, neighbors, and family members about how she should parent her child.

Perhaps this was because she was an older mother who had never had children before. Perhaps it was because of the severity of the boy's impairments. Sally patiently took it all in when medical experts told her the boy would likely never walk and that she might have to place him in an institution one day.

In her heart, though, she was sure Anton was going to be all right. She had a sense of certainty that she'd be all right, too. From early on in his life, she learned as much as she could from his health-care professionals, especially the physical, occupational, and speech therapists, about how best to help her son grow and develop. She also learned to be selective about which suggestions to implement and when to rely on her own judgment instead. As expert as the professionals were in their fields, she figured she was the real expert on Anton.

Years later, he defied the early predictions and now walks on his own with a walker. She walks by his side, proudly, as his strongest advocate. She knows that there are still some people in their lives who doubt his capabilities, and hers. But she and Anton will keep moving forward anyway.

No one knows your family and its needs the way you do.
Your surety and determination propel your loved ones onward.

Had he been wrong to make his mother move? In the middle of many nights, Kent worriedly reviewed the events leading up to the decision.

During just a four-month period earlier this year, his mother, Nella, fell three times and was hospitalized once for a broken leg. He was sure she was no longer safe living alone in the big old family house and pressed her hard to move into an assisted living facility close to his home. For months, she had resisted the idea, saying she wasn't ready. Eventually, though, she gave in to her oldest son's wishes.

Now, however, whenever Kent visited Nella and saw her slumped shoulders and sad look, he questioned his judgment. After six months in her new space, she still hadn't comfortably settled in. He'd pleaded with her to join the facility's exercise groups and make new friends, but she mostly isolated herself in her small room. If he hadn't already sold her old house, he might have been tempted to have her move back in.

But Kent also noticed other signs that told him he'd made the right choice. Nella was getting slower in her thoughts and movements. He'd received a few calls from the facility when she fell in the main dining room. When she seemed to be mixing up her day and night pills at times, he had asked the nurses to administer her medications. As much as she contended that she was fine and didn't need help, Kent was convinced more than ever that she needed an assisted living environment.

Now when he sees her dour look, he attributes her sadness to grieving for her lost capabilities due to aging, not just to the loss of her home. He feels sad, too, but knows that he has made the best decision he can to allow Nella to live as well and as safely as possible in these last years of her life.

We sometimes have to choose among less than ideal options on behalf
of our aging parents. Use your best judgment, balancing safety and
lifestyle concerns, even if your parents are not in full agreement.

CHAPTER 28

Moral Compass

> *One's philosophy is not best expressed in words; it is*
> *expressed in the choices one makes . . . and the choices*
> *we make are ultimately our responsibility.*
> —Eleanor Roosevelt

One of the greatest satisfactions we derive from caring for a loved one is the sense of being true to our moral values. Caregiving feels like the right thing to do. It resonates with our sense of honor, fairness, and goodness. We grow through assuming this important role. We come to view ourselves as giving and forgiving, sacrificing and compassionate. We carry out our caregiving mission with peace in our hearts that lasts long after the caregiving ends.

Every morning when Beatrice awoke, she'd take a deep breath and promise herself that she would not become impatient and irritable with her mother, who suffered from dementia.

Then by the end of each day, she would have broken that promise and would feel guilty and miserable. This was especially disheartening because she adored her mother. They'd been close all her life. Beatrice was actually grateful for the opportunity to care for her. She had left her job and moved into her mother's house to be her full-time caregiver.

Her mother's dementia had worsened, so that she could not do much on her own. Beatrice began the day eager to help her shower, dress, and eat breakfast. When her mother saw her and smiled, Beatrice's heart filled with joy. Later, they might go out for a pleasant walk or do some shopping. After dinner, the problems began. Her mother got disoriented, frightened, and angry. Beatrice had to struggle to change her and get her ready for bed. Sometimes, her mother screamed at her and accused her of stealing or wanting to harm her. This was always when Beatrice lost her temper and then regretted it. She knew her mother couldn't help what was happening to her.

Beatrice scheduled an appointment with her mother's doctor to discuss her mother's deterioration. She also considered hiring someone to help for a couple of hours each evening. Most importantly, she considered her feelings of gratefulness. When the next evening approached, as she watched her mother's behavior alter, she reminded herself of those feelings and her eagerness to care for her mother. She was able to avoid her own impatience and anger more successfully by focusing on her gratitude and her desire to be a loving caregiver.

When caregiving challenges arise, we do well to take the time to remember our values, get in touch with our feelings, and keep our perspective.

Now that Olivia's father was dying and she was sitting by his side, she couldn't help thinking about what kind of life he had led.

It had taken her years of therapy to admit that he'd been an alcoholic and to recognize how that had affected her. At this point, he'd had dementia for some years and was in the final stages of liver disease. He was no longer the sometimes unpredictable, unreliable, and frightening drunken man of her childhood. He was an old man in a hospital bed receiving hospice care.

Despite a slew of bad memories, Olivia found herself focusing on the good ones. Her father had been so much fun at times. He'd breeze into their childhood home and suddenly there would be energy, joy, and activity. At those times, he would be interested in his three children and what each was doing. His encouragement made them feel as if they could do anything. He was a wonderful dad on those occasions.

Olivia could see what her father's addiction had done to him and to all his important relationships. She felt deeply sad about that. Yet, as she looked at him wasting away, what she ultimately felt was her deep love for him and a big wave of compassion. He had done his best. He had loved her.

When we choose love, compassion, and forgiveness, we can let go of pain and bring a sense of peace to our lives.

Sandra could understand her friends' concerns.

They had seen her longtime husband break her heart eight years ago when he announced he was leaving her for a younger woman. They supported her through her divorce and helped her recover emotionally afterward. They had even set up dates for her with new men, when she was ready. Now it boggled their minds that she would invite her ex-husband to move back into their old home. It actually upset them.

When Sandra explained to them calmly and patiently that he now had rapidly progressing MS and his new young wife had decided she couldn't handle the care he needed, her friends were all the more bewildered. She went on to tell them that he could no longer work and had few sources of financial or emotional support. She was willing and able to take care of him.

It wasn't that Sandra didn't still have some old feelings that he had betrayed her. She couldn't quite explain to her friends the reasons for becoming his caregiver that, in some ways, had little to do with him.

For one thing, she took her marriage vows seriously. "In sickness and health" to her was a solemn oath. For another, she didn't want the burden of his care to fall on their young adult children.

Most of all, Sandra believed in the value of caring for those who are most vulnerable in this world. She had always seen this as her purpose on earth, even if it wasn't a popular sentiment or something she often articulated to others. The fact that this once-powerful, now fragile man was previously her husband was just a small part of the story. She rose to the occasion to relieve suffering, his included.

Our moral values propel us through difficult passages in our lives. It is better to do what we believe is right than to give in to expedience or popular opinion.

Fred's wife, Melinda, had agreed to take care of his mother, Lillian, now that she had moved in with them.

They had the space ever since the kids had moved out. From Fred's perspective, all was going according to plan. He assumed that Melinda, who didn't work outside the home, had a little more on her plate with his mother there, but that she still had plenty of time to take care of her responsibilities and have time to herself. When they all sat down to dinner together, Fred would ask them both how it was going, and both would politely say that things were fine.

Fred began to notice that Melinda wasn't very talkative after dinner when the two of them were alone. After asking her what was wrong several times and getting a shrug in response, he pushed the issue. When Melinda finally spoke up, Fred was surprised to hear how unhappy she was.

Melinda cried, admitting that she couldn't help feeling resentment about caring for his mother. They weren't close, and Lillian was fairly demanding of her time. She seemed to resent Melinda spending time with friends or even running errands. Melinda hadn't expected caregiving to be so difficult. She was longing for time to herself, especially now that the kids were gone. Instead, she felt as if she had another child to care for, and she felt terribly guilty about not wanting to do it.

Fred gave Melinda a hug and assured her that they would figure out what to do. He apologized for assuming things were going well. He thanked her for her honesty. They decided to hire an aide to spend some time with Lillian so that Melinda could have time to herself, and they discussed the plan and Melinda's needs with Lillian. Lillian was more receptive than they'd expected. They agreed to have more conversations about how things were going as time passed. Everyone felt relieved.

Sometimes doing the right thing means finding the balance between your own needs and the needs of a loved one. An honest assessment with caring family members helps create a sustainable situation that works best for everyone.

After months of being the sole caregiver for her mother who had breast cancer, Gwendolyn felt herself becoming upset.

She loved her mother and wanted to take her to her radiation therapy appointments and on supermarket runs. But it galled her that her brother and sister were helping so little. She knew that her siblings assumed that—since she didn't have a spouse or children and they did—she was more available to help her mother. While that was true, she felt as if they were taking her for granted, even using her.

When she'd asked her sister, Giselle, for help, Giselle had said she would try, but then she became sidetracked by her own family's needs. Gwendolyn's brother, Kurt, had been less cooperative from the beginning, flatly declining because he and their mother had never gotten along well. His dismissive tone had made Gwendolyn angry.

She decided to write them both a letter, appealing to them on moral grounds that she knew they'd understand—basic fairness and justice. Their parents had always taught them that, though life wasn't always just, they needed to be fair in all their dealings with others to demonstrate respect and goodwill. Gwendolyn embraced those values. In her letter, she reminded her sister and brother of the family's principles and stated that their choices were purposely or inadvertently unfair to her.

Both Giselle and Kurt responded by calling her directly. Giselle was apologetic; she said she hadn't realized that she was hurting Gwendolyn. She committed to taking on some of the caregiving tasks. Kurt, too, said he hadn't taken into account that he was not being fair to Gwendolyn when he resisted taking care of their mother. He, too, said he'd try harder because he wanted to do the right thing. Their responses gratified Gwendolyn. She knew they would not do as much for their mother as she did, but she was glad they wanted to at least attempt to be fair to her.

Fairness is an important dynamic in family relationships. When we treat our siblings and other relatives fairly during a time of family caregiving, we honor them and greatly strengthen our connections to them.

Resources

As caregiving—and caregivers' needs— has gained greater visibility, many caregiver organizations and resources have been created. There are, in fact, so many outlets for information and assistance that knowing where to turn for help can be daunting. This section provides a step-by-step guide to learning about your loved one's condition and getting the aid you need to be an effective caregiver. In addition to these national resources, you'll also want to find local resources in your community.

Step One: Educate Yourself about Your Loved One's Condition
Different diseases and circumstances pose different challenges to individuals and their family caregivers. An important first step on your caregiving journey is to learn about your loved one's condition to best prepare yourself for caregiving now and in the months and years ahead. The following resources can provide you with the basics. Always confer with your loved one's medical providers to learn more specific information.

ASTHMA
American Lung Association (www.lung.org; 800-LUNGUSA). This national advocacy organization's website has information about the causes, treatments, and long-term management of asthma, as well as an online support community for patients and caregivers.

American Academy of Allergy, Asthma & Immunology (www .aaaai.org). This professional organization for allergists provides basic information about asthma and a referral service for allergy specialists in your community.

AUTISM

Autism Speaks (www.autismspeaks.org; 888-288-4762—for English speakers, 888-772-9050—for Spanish speakers). This advocacy and science organization provides information about the different conditions within the autism spectrum and the latest treatment methods. It offers the services of an Autism Response Team—specially trained advisers to guide family members over the phone to appropriate services.

ARTHRITIS

Arthritis Foundation (www.arthritis.org; 404-872-7100). This national organization's website covers the wide range of arthritic conditions and treatments. It offers an online support community for patients and family caregivers.

BRAIN INJURY

Brain Injury Association of America (www.biausa.org; 703-584-862). This national organization's website has medical and advocacy information, including guidance for family caregivers coping with their loved one's needs at different stages of recovery.

CANCER

American Cancer Society (www.cancer.org; 800-227-2345). Cancer information specialists are available to answer your questions through this organization's National Cancer Information Center. It also offers online support communities for patients and family caregivers, as well as MyLifeLine.org, a program for developing your own web-based social support network.

National Cancer Institute (www.cancer.gov; 800-4-CANCER). This U.S. federal agency offers extensive information on cancer and living well with the disease. Its website has a section with coping tips for family caregivers.

CEREBRAL PALSY

United Cerebral Palsy (www.ucp.org; 800-872-5827). This national organization's website has an extensive section with information for family caregivers on coping, assistive technologies, financial advice, and online and local resources.

CHRONIC PAIN

American Chronic Pain Association (www.theacpa.org; 800-533-3231). The website has information on the range of pain conditions, treatments, and pain management programs.

DEMENTIA

Alzheimer's Association (www.alz.org; 800-272-3900). This national association offers basic information, an extensive network of local family caregiver trainings and support groups, and online message boards.

Alzheimer's Foundation of America (www.alzfdn.org; 866-232-8484). A consortium of professional organizations, it offers a national help line run by social workers to answer caregivers' questions.

The Association for Frontotemporal Degeneration (www.theaftd.org; 866-507-7222). This association offers in-person and telephone support groups for family caregivers of different ages, as well as online Facebook and Yahoo groups.

DIABETES

American Diabetes Association (www.diabetes.org; 800-342-2383). This national organization's website has basic information, meal and exercise plans, and advice for caregivers about family communication and coping.

HEART DISEASE

American Heart Association (www.heart.org; 800-242-8721). Its "Support Network" is an online community for patients and caregivers. The website also has printable handouts on caregiver self-care, burnout, and family communication.

INTELLECTUAL DISABILITIES
The Arc (www.thearc.org; 800-433-5255). The website has information on the types of intellectual disabilities, employment resources for individuals, and online support groups for siblings of different ages.

KIDNEY DISEASE
National Kidney Foundation (www.kidney.org; 855-653-2273). This national organization offers information for patients, family caregivers, and health-care professionals on kidney dialysis, transplantation, nutrition, and financial assistance.

MENTAL ILLNESS
Mental Health America (www.mentalhealthamerica.net; 800-969-6642). This advocacy organization's website has dozens of articles on mental health diagnoses and topics, including being an effective caregiver and fostering self-determination as a caregiver.

NAMI: National Alliance on Mental Illness (www.nami.org; 800-950-6264). The website has information on schizophrenia, bipolar disorder, obsessive-compulsive disorder, and nine other mental illnesses. "NAMI Family-to-Family" is a free, twelve-session educational program for family caregivers. NAMI also sponsors local family support groups throughout the country.

MULTIPLE SCLEROSIS
National MS Society (www.nationalmssociety.org; 800-344-4867). The website features information on the disease and its treatments, as well as a guide for caregivers with tips on emotional support, hiring help, and financial planning.

PARKINSON'S DISEASE
National Parkinson Foundation (www.parkinson.org; 800-473-4636). Its "Helpline" is staffed by knowledgeable health-care professionals who provide information and guidance. The website has information on the neurological condition and advice for caregivers at different stages of the disease's progression.

Parkinson's Disease Foundation (www.pdf.org; 800-457-6676). This national organization provides information and advice for care partners to improve family communication and seek support. The organization also offers a help line.

STROKE

American Stroke Association (www.strokeassociation.org; 888-478-7653). The website has information on the causes of and treatments for stroke and downloadable caregiver resources. Its "Support Network" is an online social network for stroke survivors and caregivers.

National Stroke Association (www.stroke.org; 800-787-6537). The "Careliving Guide" gives family members information on setting up a loved one's care team and managing recovery. Its "Careliving Community" is an online social network for stroke survivors and caregivers.

Step Two: Explore the Three Circles of Caregiver Support

Three circles of emotional and logistical support are vital for family caregivers.

Initially, most caregivers depend on such support from the *first circle*—immediate family members. As those sons, daughters, spouses, brothers, and sisters step up to help an ill or disabled loved one and each other, stronger bonds form and the family perseveres.

If immediate family support is not available or caregiving demands increase to the point where more help is needed, then caregivers generally look to the *second circle*—extended family members, friends, and community members. Every family and community has its methods and traditions for assisting members in need, including those engaged in caring for loved ones. Here are some ideas for garnering second-circle support:

Local religious institutions. Many churches, synagogues, and mosques have developed "senior ministries" or other programs specifically to support family caregivers. These programs often consist of providing meals when a loved one is in the hospital ("the covered casserole brigade"); institution-based, in-person caregiver support groups; lay counseling (e.g., Stephen Ministries); and prayer groups. Congregants need only request assistance.

Create your family's own caregiving website. Several organizations offer a way to create a secure website specific to your family's medical and caregiving situation. These family websites make it easier to share information with and coordinate the efforts of your second circle.

CarePages (https://carepages.com) allows you to create a free patient blog to convey information to family members and friends. It also has information on common medical problems and unmoderated discussion forums on health topics and caregiving.

CareZone (https://carezone.com) has software to enable you to create a website for sharing a to-do list, schedule, notes, symptom journal, medication list, contact information, and photos.

CaringBridge (www.caringbridge.org) allows you share medical updates, coordinate everyday help, and convey messages among friends and family members.

eCare Diary (www.ecarediary.com) has a Care Diary for maintaining a calendar, storing and sharing medical and medication records, and starting a blog. Its website also contains articles, radio shows, and webinars on caregiving.

Lotsa Helping Hands (www.lotsahelpinghands.com) enables caregivers to create family websites whose main features are a care calendar and a means for communicating updates and support.

If the support from the first and second circles is not sufficient, then many caregivers come to rely on the *third circle*—health-care and social service professionals. Most American communities have an infrastructure of available professional services, including home health aides, senior centers, adult day-care programs, case managers, social workers, physical therapists, mental health counselors, primary care physicians, and medical specialists. Without knowing about particular professionals or agencies, finding the right professional care team members can be confusing. Here are some ideas for best utilizing this third-circle support:

ElderCare Locator (www.eldercare.gov). This is a public service of the U.S. Administration on Aging. By entering your zip code into its search function, this website provides contact information for the Area Agency on Aging (AAA) in your community. Case managers from the AAA can conduct an evaluation of your loved one and suggest professional services, including home health-care agencies, adult day-care programs, and free, in-person caregiver support groups. The AAA may also provide funding for services for families that meet income eligibility criteria. The website also has links to informative publications and national organizations.

Call 2-1-1 (www.211.org). In many American communities, you can learn about local health-care and social services, as well as food, disaster assistance, housing, and other resources, by calling 2-1-1. The information provided is free and confidential.

Step Three: Learn How to Thrive in Your Caregiving Role
Many national organizations, such as those listed below, are devoted to caregiver support, education, advocacy, and research. Many offer information on a wide array of caregiving subjects, online support groups, and helplines.

AARP (www.aarp.org). With 37 million members, AARP has launched several major initiatives in recent years to aid family caregivers of older adults. AARP Caregiving Resource Center (www.aarp.org/caregiving) contains information and tools on planning, coping, grief and loss, legal and financial issues, end-of-life care, and many other subjects. The AARP Caregiving App, available through the AARP Health Tools web page (www.aarp.org/tools), helps manage medications, keep a list of contacts, and store photos and other information. The AARP Rx App, also available through the Health Tools page, provides drug and health information and provides a system for organizing medications and doctors' instructions. The AARP Take Care blog (blog.aarp.org/category/take-care/) covers current news and topics of pertinence to family caregivers. AARP also offers an online community for caregivers (https://community.aarp .org/t5/Caregiving/bd-p/bf41).

ARCH National Respite Network (www.archrespite.org; 919-490-5577). This national organization promotes respite services for family caregivers. Its National Respite Locator (www.archrespite.org /respitelocator) helps identify respite providers and funding for respite in your community.

Caregiver Action Network (www.caregiveraction.org; 202-454-3970). Its "Family Caregiver Toolbox" has information on effective communication with health-care providers, financial planning, technology, caregiver depression, and other key topics. Its "Story Project" allows caregivers to tell their own stories and read those of other caregivers. It also sponsors an online discussion forum.

Caregiver Briefcase (http://www.apa.org/pi/about/publications /caregivers). This website, developed by the American Psychological Association for psychologists, contains information on caregiving facts, practice, research, education, advocacy, and resources that is helpful to family caregivers.

CaringInfo (www.caringinfo.org). A website run by the National Hospice and Palliative Care Organization, it contains information on advance care planning, caregiving, hospice and palliative care, and grief and loss.

Center for Parent Information and Resources (www.parentcenter hub.org). This online clearinghouse of information for parents about caring for children with disabilities contains sections on family supports including advocating for your child and getting ready for health-care and financial planning when your child turns eighteen.

Easter Seals (www.easterseals.com). This national organization de-voted to helping individuals with disabilities and special needs has created resources for family caregivers, including informative articles, a "Military Caregiving Webinar Series," and a "Caregiver's Spokesperson Network."

Family Caregiver Alliance (www.caregiver.org; 800-445-8106). One of the leading caregiving support organizations, its website contains in-formation on in-home caregiving, long distance caregiving, advanced illnesses, and the post-caregiving period. It has multiple online sup-port groups (including one for LGBT caregivers) and sponsors several California-based in-person support groups (including one conducted in Spanish). Its "Family Care Navigator" (www.caregiver.org/family -care-navigator) provides information about local caregiver support programs throughout the United States.

National Alliance for Caregiving (www.caregiving.org). A coalition of national caregiver organizations and the leading advocacy organiza-tion, its website contains research briefs on many aspects of caregiving, including long distance caregivers, rural caregivers, and Hispanic fam-ily caregivers.

National Resource Center on LGBT Aging (www.lgbtagingcenter .org; 212-741-2247). Its website contains downloadable materials on the emotional and legal challenges of LGBT caregiving, as well as respite, long distance caregiving, and many other topics.

Next Step in Care (www.nextstepincare.org). A program of the United Hospital Fund of New York, its website contains caregiver guides and videos on managing medical visits, medications, and end-of-life planning, as well as advocating for your loved one in a variety of health-care settings (e.g., surgery, rehabilitation, emergency room, home care).

Rosalynn Carter Institute for Caregiving (www.rosalynncarter.org; 229-928-1234). This advocacy and support organization sponsors caregiver trainings in the state of Georgia and nationally. Its website contains a very extensive listing of caregiver resources (www.rosalynncarter.org/caregiver_resources/). Its "Operation Family Caregiver" (www.operationfamilycaregiver.org) coaches military families to successfully cope with the difficulties they face when veterans return home.

Veterans Affairs Caregiver Support Program (www.caregiver.va.gov; 855-260-3274). Among its many services are a "Caregiver Support Line," "Caregiver Tool Box" (containing checklists and diagnosis care sheets), and a "Peer Support Mentoring Program." "Caregiver Support Coordinators," located at sites throughout the country, are available to guide military caregivers to the appropriate VA services.

Well Spouse Association (www.wellspouse.org; 800-838-0879). This national organization, dedicated to the well-being of spousal caregivers, sponsors in-person and telephone support groups, respite events, and an annual national conference. Its website contains a well spouse bill of rights, a description of the caregiver journey, and copies of the organization's *Mainstay* newsletter.

References for Quotations

Chapter 1, page 1: "The Poet's Tale; The Birds of Killingworth"

Chapter 2, page 7: http://tinybuddha.com/wisdom-quotes/if-you-are
-patient-in-one-moment-of-anger-you-will-escape-one-hundred-days-
of-sorrow/

Chapter 3, page 15: http://www.bbcamerica.com/anglophenia/2014/09
/happy-birthday-t-s-eliot-20-quotes/

Chapter 4, page 22: http://positivemed.com/2012/06/10/we-must-be
-willing-to-let-go-of-the-life-we-have-planned/

Chapter 5, page 28: *Following the Equator: A Journey Around the World*, by
Mark Twain

Chapter 6, page 35: http://www.beliefnet.com/Quotes/Relationships/N
/No-Title/This-world-is-nothing-but-a-school-of-love.aspx?q=Marriage

Chapter 7, page 43: NPR Interview: http://www.npr.org/2005/04/04
/4568464/in-giving-i-connect-with-others

Chapter 8, page 50: http://www.keepinspiring.me/quotes-about-creativity
-imagination-and-innovation/

Chapter 9, page 56: *The Irony of American History*, by Reinhold Niebuhr
(1952)

Chapter 10, page 64: https://www.lds.org/general-conference/1989/10
/remembrance-and-gratitude?lang=eng#watch=video

Chapter 11, page 71: http://thinkexist.com/quotation/there_is_a
_sacredness_in_tears-they_are_not_the/149959.html

Chapter 12, page 78: http://gretchenrubin.com/happiness_project/2013 /11/feeling-lonely-consider-trying-these-7-strategies/

Chapter 13, page 87: *Mansfield Park,* by Jane Austen (chapter 42)

Chapter 14, page 95: www.brainyquote.com/quotes/quotes/j/johannwolf 140778.html

Chapter 15, page 103: "Hypocrites You Always Have With You," by Kurt Vonnegut (1980)

Chapter 16, page 109: http://dalailamacenter.org/blog-post/can-you -teach-compassion

Chapter 17, page 116: http://inspirationalquotes.gallery/once-we-accept -our-limits-we-go-beyond-them/

Chapter 18, page 125: whatwillmatter.com/2013/01/quotes-posters-a -caring-heart-that-listens-is-often-more-valued-than-an-intelligent -mind-that-talks-from-love-quotes-and-sayings-2/

Chapter 19, page 133: ttp://www.ellafitzgerald.com/about/quotes.html

Chapter 20, page 141: http://www.brainyquote.com/quotes/quotes/w /waltwhitma384665.html

Chapter 21, page 149: http://tinybuddha.com/wisdom-quotes/hope-is -being-able-to-see-that-there-is-light-despite-all-of-the-darkness/

Chapter 22, page 155: *Slouching Towards Bethlehem,* by Joan Didion (1968)

Chapter 23, page 161: http://www.huffingtonpost.com/2014/05/28 /maya-angelou-love_n_5405609.html

Chapter 24, page 167: http://thinkexist.com/quotation/two_things _inspire_me_to_awe-the_starry_heavens/15628.html

Chapter 25, page 173: *Power and Innocence: A Search for the Sources of Violence,* by Rollo May (1972)

Chapter 26, page 179: http://www.bbc.co.uk/irish/proverbs/english/

Chapter 27, page 188: "Self-Reliance," by Ralph Waldo Emerson (1841)

Chapter 28, page 194: *You Learn by Living,* by Eleanor Roosevelt (1960)

Index

About the Authors

Barry J. Jacobs, PsyD, is a clinical psychologist, family therapist, and the Director of Behavioral Sciences for the Crozer-Keystone Family Medicine Residency Program in Springfield, Pennsylvania. He is the author of *The Emotional Survival Guide for Caregivers—Looking After Yourself and Your Family While Helping an Aging Parent*. Dr. Jacobs has given more than 400 presentations on family caregiving for family caregivers, community groups, and medical and mental health professionals. He is the national spokesperson on caregiving for the American Heart Association and an honorary board member of the Well Spouse Association. He has served on the expert panel for the Caregiver Crisis Great Challenge for TEDMED.com and as a board member of the Collaborative Family Healthcare Association. He has held adjunct faculty positions with the Temple University School of Medicine, the University of Pennsylvania School of Nursing, and the Department of Psychology of the Philadelphia College of Osteopathic Medicine. A columnist on family caregiving topics for AARP.org, Dr. Jacobs received his bachelor's degree from Brown University and his doctorate in psychology from Hahnemann/Widener Universities.

Julia L. Mayer, PsyD, is a clinical psychologist who has been counseling individuals and couples for almost 25 years. Dr. Mayer has a private practice in Media, Pennsylvania, where she specializes in women's issues, including caregiving and other relationship concerns. She has held adjunct teaching positions at the Institute for Graduate Clinical Psychology of Widener University and in Widener University's undergraduate programs. She was also an instructor for the Master's Program in Creative Arts Therapy at Hahnemann University, teaching courses on human development and psychoanalytic theory. Her novel, *A Fleeting State of Mind*, was published in 2014. Dr. Mayer received her bachelor's degree from the University of Pennsylvania and her doctorate in psychology from Widener University.

Drs. Jacobs and Mayer have written previously together for WebMD and HealthCentral. They have been married for more than 25 years and have two adult children.